Lir

'it

Carl and other writings

by

Mirabelle Maslin

with an appendix by Dr W N Taylor

Augur Press

CARL AND OTHER WRITINGS
Copyright © Mirabelle Maslin 2000-2005

The moral right of the author has been asserted

Author of:
Beyond the Veil
Tracy

British Library Cataloguing in Publication Data.
A catalogue record for this book is available from the British Library.

ISBN 0-9549551-2-9

First published 2005 by
Augur Press
Delf House,
52 Penicuik Road,
Roslin,
Midlothian EH25 9LH
United Kingdom

Printed by Lightning Source

Carl and other writings

With thanks to my editors

Contents

For all who struggle with their emotional problems.

Introduction

I am a therapist with many years' experience of helping people with emotional and relationship problems. I wrote the following stories and essays over a period of several years. After making the decision to bring these together, I have been asked to write something that will help the many people in our society who have been sexually abused – people who often feel isolated and unable to speak about their experiences. This collection has much in it that documents abusive events, together with the contexts in which these events may occur. Although written as fiction, much of the content of the stories is true. I have added a number of other writings which I hope will be of help. Although many problems are shared by sexually abused people, I believe it is of paramount importance to help each person to develop individually. Sexually abusive events invariably result in the attenuation of the development of the personality of the victim. The mechanisms whereby this takes place, and the contexts within which they occur, are many and varied, so that a single kind of approach could never hope to address the need of each person.

The book is split into three parts.

Part I

The first story – *Carl* – is based on the life of a person who became an abuser. *Aumbries* is a reflection on the loss of spiritual respect in our culture. *Dates* documents a sexually abusive situation. *The Greenhouse* is a reflection on life through two generations of childhood history. *Cock o' the North* looks at the life of a child who is being treated in a way that makes her very vulnerable to sexual abuse. *Fried Onions* encourages thought about life, death and regret. *The Psychiatrist* is an account of sexual abuse, portrayed largely through the experience of the child.

Part II

I wrote *Sexual abuse of children* and also *Recovered memories* at the request of a former juror in a well-publicised case of sexual abuse – that was heard in the High Court in Edinburgh. *An adult survivor's perspective* enables the sexually abused reader to feel validated in the struggles of daily life, and provides pointers to how to strengthen and consolidate confidence in appropriate self-expression. This includes my response to the *Call for Evidence at stage I of the Bill SP30 – Protection of Children and Prevention of Sexual Offences (Scotland)*. I have included *Addictions and 'cold turkey'* because many of those who have been sexually abused suffer symptoms of addiction until they are helped to speak about their suffering.

The book finishes with a relevant essay, by Dr W N Taylor, who is a retired psychiatrist.

Part I

Carl

1.

Carl had always wanted a car. He had wanted a car as far back as he could remember. When he had been small, he had wanted a car like the one his father had, but now he was older he wanted a different kind of car. His ideas about the exact model and specification changed almost every day, but that was all right. With every day that passed he learned as much as he could, and he was refining his ideas as he went along – he was certain about this.

He couldn't wait to be seventeen, when he would be able to apply for his provisional driving licence and get his parents to pay for lessons. He had tried to speak to them about this on many occasions, but they seemed uninterested and dismissive. Their attitude made him feel angry – very angry indeed. Could they not see that this was the only thing that mattered? He felt so angry that he wanted to break things. He wanted to smash things... to destroy. If only he could learn to drive and get his own car, he was sure that he would feel fine.

Carl lived with his parents in an expensive bungalow in a secluded area next to a private swimming pool. All the windows had leaded lights. He hated this. It meant that you could not see out of the windows properly, and you felt trapped. It seemed to him like a large wire mesh all over the windows. But what else can you expect? he thought. After all, this place is just like a prison.

Carl didn't really know what a prison was like. His only source of information had been a TV programme about the USA, and some films he had half watched. But he certainly felt shut in and trapped. Sometimes he thought it was strange to feel like this amongst the expensive floor coverings, the antique furniture and the up-market fittings. Surely there weren't things like that in a prison. There certainly hadn't been any on the film footage he had seen. But it hardly mattered what was here, the main thing was that he *felt* as if he were in a prison, and that was all that mattered to him right now.

He tried to recall when he had first noticed the wire mesh on the windows, but failed. The way he felt these days assured him that it had *always* been there, making sure he was trapped. He certainly remembered the day when he noticed there were other kinds of windows. That was the day when he learned for certain that not everyone lived in a prison. It was the day his mother had taken him to the private nursery.

One morning when he got out of bed to find his soldiers to play with, his mother had said, 'Today you are going to the nursery, so get your clothes on.'

That word 'nursery'... what did it mean? It was obviously something to do with somewhere you went. He tried to follow his mother, asking her what a nursery was, but the question didn't come out right, and all she did was snarl at him, saying, 'Get your clothes on... *now!*' He felt his legs begin to wobble, and his whole body started to shake, so he ran back to his room and clutched his favourite soldier – the one with a gun in each hand.

He looked at the chair where his clothes were invariably laid out, and found a grey shirt that was entirely unfamiliar. It felt stiff and uncomfortable when he tried to put it on. He got his arms through the sleeves and managed some of the lower buttons, but the top buttons defeated him, and he turned to the dark grey shorts. Thank goodness there was elastic round the back of them. This meant that he did not have to wrestle with the fastenings. The socks were easy, and so were the shoes.

Miraculously he had already managed to master the tying of laces. Although he was only four years old, he could do them up. At least with laces you could see what you had in your hands, not like trying to do up top buttons. Although the moves for tying a bow were quite complicated, he had managed to teach himself what to do by investigating the bows on ribbons of the cuddly toys he had in his room.

Those toys were anathema to him. They were kept on a high shelf, and he wasn't really allowed to touch them. But at night, when he couldn't sleep, he had stood on a chair and reached them down to investigate their bows. This had been for a very important reason. He had thought that if he could learn to tie bows on shoes like Father did, then he too would be able to go out of the house, drive a car, and disappear down the road.

His father always wore slippers in the house. As soon as he came home, he took off his shoes at the door and put his slippers on; and when he left the house, he took his slippers off, put his shoes on, tied the laces, and then he was gone.

The slippers were made of soft materials, and he could creep along and take Carl by surprise at any moment, if he let his attention slip. When he was very young, he had soon learned to play with less than half of his attention. Most of his awareness was taken up with listening out for tiny sounds that might be important, or even crucial, and watching out for changes in lighting and shadows. This expedient led to a considerable reduction in the fear and pain he had to suffer while his father was around, and was well worth the energy he invested in it.

When he was younger, Carl had assumed that the slippers were entirely for the purpose of destroying his games and his peace of mind, but now he was not so sure. Maybe they had that function in part, but also maybe the slippers had something to do with the well-being of the floor coverings. After all, he too had to wear slippers in the house, and he was never given the idea that he could terrorise anyone.

Mother was forever referring to her Persian carpet; and when she had her high heels on, ready to go out, she would walk round that carpet, keeping to the stained floorboards.

Carl struggled with his shirt buttons again. There was no point in looking for Ivy, his sister. For one thing, she wouldn't be there. She would have left with Father already. For another, she wouldn't help him with anything. He had long ago given up trying to get any help from her. He used to think she wouldn't help him just so that things would be even worse for him, but later he began to wonder if she *couldn't* help him.

There was something really funny about her legs. They didn't work properly. When his father hit him, his legs often felt just like Ivy's looked, but whenever he went to the mirror to check, they seemed the same as usual. Ivy's legs were bent sideways at her knees, and she couldn't walk properly. In fact, she didn't walk at all... she lurched.

Ivy went to a special place in the daytime. Father took her there. Carl didn't know where the special place was. All he knew was that she went there. He had heard them talking about it.

One more try with buttons, he decided, then he would give up and put the grey jumper on. Having failed again with the buttons, he ended up with the V of the jumper behind his neck, and had to start all over again.

By this time he could hear his mother shouting for him. 'Carl! Come here! This instant! You'll be late!'

He knew what 'Come here, this instant!' meant, and he steeled himself for the inevitable thwack across the side of his head, accompanied by its

3

attendant temporary fog and ringing sounds.

He rushed into the hall just in time to avert that course of events. His mother dropped his coat by his feet and opened the door. Somehow he managed to get his arms through the sleeves with the first try, and he climbed over the doorstep and on to the flight of uneven stone steps that led down. At the bottom, the flight joined the drive that led out on to the road, but which also led back to the garage under the house.

As he stumbled along beside his mother, who was now taking giant strides down the road, the word 'nursery' came back into his mind. What this was he would no doubt soon find out.

2.

Carl's mother took him to a very large house that looked nothing at all like her house – the bungalow where he lived. For one thing it had a huge garden that you walked past to get to it. Then, when you got to the house, it seemed to reach right up to the sky. He afterwards learned that this was because it had an upstairs, with attics above that. But that was years later.

His mother pressed a button, and he could hear a ringing sound from inside the house. It was different from the one he heard when she hit his head, but had some similarity. The door was soon opened by a woman. Carl noticed that her legs were straight, and not bent like Ivy's. He was not sure if this would be the kind of person who hit him, or the kind who wouldn't help him. He was vaguely aware that you couldn't tell just from the shape of the legs, but he didn't know why. He would have to wait and see.

The woman smiled.

'Carl Middleton,' his mother snapped, and thrust him through the open door.

Carl nearly felt flat as he tripped on something, but much to his surprise the woman caught him. Well, he worked that out later. What happened was that he thought he would feel himself crash on the floor, but he didn't reach it. Instead there was something soft and warm, and he gradually worked out that it was some arms.

He heard his mother say, 'I'll be back at twelve.' After that, the woman, with her soft arm things still on him, leaned on the door to shut it.

Carl stared around him. He was in a huge place, and there were lots of people. People never came to where he lived with his mother and father and Ivy. The only other places he knew were shops, where he sometimes went with his mother. At the shops he saw lots of other people, of all different shapes and sizes. He also saw them on his father's TV, but that was only by accident – he wasn't really allowed to see them there. Then he realised that most of the people here were the same size as himself. That struck him as being odd, when he compared it with being at the shops.

The woman with the soft arms was speaking to him.

'Carl, would you like to take your coat off?' she asked.

Carl wasn't quite sure what that meant, but he knew the 'coat off' bit, and obediently removed his coat.

The soft arms woman went on. 'Come with me, and I'll show you

5

where to hang it up.'

He followed her to one side of the huge place, where she showed him a row of pegs sticking out of the wall, together with a row of pictures underneath.

'This one is yours,' she said, pointing to a peg with a picture of a car underneath it. That car was not like his father's, but he had seen one like it on the road when he walked to the shops with his mother, and he had never forgotten it. She took his coat from him, and hung it on the peg above the car. There was something odd about all this. Carl realised that she had not snatched the coat from him, or ordered him to do anything. He felt confused and uncomfortable. There was something very strange about this place. He grabbed at the front of his shorts.

The warm arms woman plucked him off the ground and hurried through a door. With his legs dangling, he knew that something painful was about to happen, and he clutched himself more tightly.

'Let me help you,' she said, as she put him down with his feet back on the floor.

He continued to clutch himself. He had screwed his eyes tight shut, but now he opened them. He was in a small room with a toilet that was the wrong size. It was only about half the size of the one he was used to.

'Let me help you,' she repeated.

Afterwards, she took his hand in hers, and showed him where they would wash their hands.

When they went back into the huge place, a number of children, none of whom had coats on, were waiting.

The warm arms woman addressed them. 'Now, children, this is Carl Middleton. Say hello to him.'

'Hello, Carl,' the children chorused.

Carl was astonished. He had never been in a place like this before. People in shops nearly always had their coats on, and they hardly ever spoke to him. Added to that, they were mostly big. Here, nearly all the people were the same size as he was, they had no coats on, *and* they were speaking to him. They weren't shouting at him like his mother and father did. They were speaking to him.

The woman was saying words again. 'Shall we take Carl to the playroom?' she asked the children.

'Yes!' they chorused.

'But wait a minute, he doesn't know your names yet.'

The children stood in a row in front of him, and took it in turns to tell him their names.

The woman smiled. 'That was very good, children,' she said. 'Now, we must remember that Carl will take a little while before he remembers your names. So help him with that, won't you?'

'Yes – we – will!' they said, in unison; and they ran through a large doorway.

Carl and the woman followed them, and he found himself in another huge place. This place had enormous windows, and *none of them had wire on.* He was in a house, and none of the windows had wire.

Carl stared and stared at the windows. He forgot the woman, he forgot the children, and he forgot the room. All he could see was the windows... the huge windows... the windows without wire on them. There was something else too... it was not dark in this room. In fact it was as light as if he were outside.

He heard the woman speaking to him.

'Carl,' she said. 'Carl?'

He turned his head towards the sound of her voice, and discovered that her head was next to his. He jumped.

'Oh, I didn't mean to startle you,' she said.

Carl looked down at her legs, and saw that they were bent; but they were bent in the way that his could bend. He looked back at her head.

'Would you like to play in the sand, or would you like to paint a picture?' she asked.

He did not understand what she was saying, so he nodded, hoping that would placate her. She stood up, took his hand, and led him across to a low table. No, it wasn't a low table. It had legs like a table, but the top was not flat. It was a kind of huge shallow sink, and it was full of a pinkish-yellow dry earth.

He felt agitated because he could see that some of the other children were putting their hands in it, and he knew that the woman would start shouting soon. His whole body stiffened, and he shut his eyes again. But there was no shouting. Instead, the woman pulled up the sleeves of his jumper and rolled up the sleeves of his shirt. Then she handed him a thing that looked like a very large yellow spoon.

'You can play with this in the sand,' she said.

He could see some of the other children had things that they were pushing into this stuff, and that everyone seemed quite calm. Cautiously, he tried to copy them.

'Yes, that's right,' said the woman. Then she walked away from him, and disappeared through the door.

Carl stirred the pinkish-yellow dry earth with his spoon thing. It was interesting to see the way this dry stuff moved, but it was of less interest than those windows. Those windows were so huge; and however carefully he studied them, he could see no sign of wire on them at all.

At length the woman returned, pushing a thing on wheels that carried a lot of mugs and plates, together with a large jug.

'Time to wash your hands, children,' she called.

That was something Carl knew about, and he knew where to go to do it too. He went with all the other children back to the sinks in that place he had been in with the woman before; and when everyone had finished, he ran back with them to where the woman was pouring something out of the jug into the mugs. The other children all sat on the floor in a circle round the woman, and he copied them. Then she handed a mug to each of them.

When Carl took a mug from the woman, he was very careful not to spill from it – very careful indeed. He took a sip, and found it tasted good – really good. He did not know what it was, but it tasted good. And now, here was a plate with a biscuit on it. The woman put it on the floor beside him. Carl could hardly believe his luck. A drink *and* a biscuit. When he had finished his drink, he ate his biscuit slowly, to make it last.

When all the mugs and plates were empty, the woman loaded them on the thing she could push along, and then she said, 'Right, children! Let's have a story.'

A story? Carl wondered to himself. He had had a story once. It was about a lorry. There were no cars in it, but it had been good all the same. His mother and father had gone out after tea one evening, and a strange woman had come before they left. She stayed in the house while he went to bed; but when he woke up in the morning she wasn't there, and no one said anything about her. Not even Ivy said anything about her. That woman had brought in her bag a book about a lorry, and she had read it to him when he was in bed. Perhaps the nursery woman was going to read a story about a lorry? He waited.

The woman went across to the wall nearest the open door, and it was then he noticed that there were a lot of books, on shelves. There seemed to be hundreds of them! She chose a book, and returned to the circle.

'Now, children,' she said. 'Open the circle to let my chair in.'

The children nearest to her shuffled to one side, and she put her chair down and sat on it.

'This book is called *The Tale of Peter Rabbit*,' she said, as she held up the picture of Peter Rabbit on the front cover. Then she began to read. 'Once upon a time, there were four little rabbits...'

After she read each page, she held the picture on the opposite page up so that everyone could see it. Carl loved the pictures. Some of them looked a little like the park he could see across the road from where he lived, when he looked through the wire mesh windows. He had even seen rabbits there, but there hadn't been any that wore a blue jacket like Peter.

He grasped some of the story too. Peter Rabbit was naughty, he learned, and got into a lot of trouble. Carl wasn't really sure what naughty was. It was certainly what he himself was, but he didn't really know what it meant. He knew what getting into trouble was, because that was always happening to him; but he didn't really understand it, except that it hurt.

The story finished, and the woman returned the book to the shelf.

When she came back to her chair, she began to make a wonderful singing sound. There were words too, something about fingers, and the other children joined in; but Carl sat with his mouth open, drinking in the wonderful singing sound that was coming from the woman. He was transfixed.

His reverie was harshly shattered by a ringing noise. He clutched his head, but curiously it wasn't hurting. The woman had stopped making the lovely sound, had got up out of her chair, and was going through the door. Carl tried to shout to her. He wanted to call to her 'don't go away', but the words got stuck in his throat, and he could scarcely breathe.

Then he heard her voice in the hall saying, 'Hello, Mrs Middleton, do come in. You're a little early, but I'll get his coat. Carl's been fine. Could you wait here a moment, please?'

He heard footsteps, and then she appeared with his coat and helped him to put it on. She took his hand, and led him to where his mother was waiting.

'Bye for now, Carl,' she said firmly. 'We'll see you again next week.'

His mother grabbed his arm and marched him through the door into the outside world. She marched him up the road, and back to the prison.

He never saw that soft warm woman again, but he never forgot her. It was because of her that he was then sure that there was something wrong where he lived – something terribly wrong.

9

3.

Carl had made a special calendar for himself. It showed how many days were left before his seventeenth birthday. Every evening when he went to bed, he would cross the day off on his special calendar.

He still attended school. He knew there had been many meetings between his parents and the Head, because he had no interest in the work they gave him there. He knew that many members of staff were angry and frustrated with him. He had recently been told that he had only one more chance. But that was irrelevant. Soon he would be seventeen, and then he would get his provisional licence and driving lessons. He would see to that. He counted the days… only thirteen more to go.

On the day of his birthday, he got out of bed, and dressed quickly. He went into his parents' room. This was something he hadn't done for a very long time. In fact the last time he had done this, he had been very small – smaller than the day his mother took him to nursery. Very early on he had discovered that going into his parents' room inevitably resulted in a lot of pain, and he stopped even thinking about it. But today he went straight there.

'Wake up!' he shouted, bending down and tearing the bedclothes from them. 'Wake up!' He grabbed his father's hair. 'A form. Get me a form. *Now!*'

His father's face grew pale, but he got out of bed, drew himself up as tall as he could, and snarled, 'Get back to your room, Carl, or it'll be the worse for you.'

Carl began to turn to leave the room; but he was conscious for the first time that he was quite a bit taller than his father, and he stood his ground.

'I'm not going until you promise to get me a form and book me the lessons,' he said belligerently.

He noticed that his mother looked frightened. He had never seen her look like this before, and it amused him. He became aware of a strange noise, and it was some time before he realised that it was coming from his body – he was laughing.

At that moment Ivy lurched into the room, and fell forward on her hands and knees. Carl picked her up and half-carried, half-dragged her back to her room, where he dumped her on her bed.

'Stay there for now!' he ordered. 'Just stay out of the way!'

On the way back through the hall, he picked up the Yellow Pages, and returned to his parents' room to find his father putting on a dressing-gown. He had seen that the bathroom door was shut, and presumed his mother was in there.

'Right, Mr Shoelaces,' Carl snapped. He thrust the Yellow Pages into his father's hands. 'Phone!'

With shaking hands, his father thumbed the pages to the section headed 'Driving Schools'.

'Phone!' Carl repeated.

'Carl,' said his father. 'They won't be open until nine. It's only seven-thirty now.'

'Go into the sitting room and sit there until nine,' Carl commanded.

Ashen-faced, his father stood up, put his feet into his slippers, collected the Yellow Pages, and made his way to the sitting room. Carl followed him and pushed him down on to one of the soft chairs – the one that was next to the phone extension. After that he sat on a firm chair – looking down at his father. Every time his father made as if to say something, he growled at him in a way that silenced him before any sound came.

At nine o'clock he motioned towards the phone, and his father lifted it and keyed a number.

'Is that the ACE Driving School? I want to book lessons for my son. Could you also tell me how he can apply for his provisional licence? ... You have an information pack? Please do send one. The name is Carl Middleton.'

Carl relaxed a little as he heard his father use *his* name, and go on to give their address and phone number.

'I'd like to book a couple of lessons,' he heard his father say.

'*Ten*,' snarled Carl, advancing to grab at his father's hair again.

'I meant to say ten,' his father told the phone hurriedly. 'Yes, I'll send the deposit today. They start in about six weeks' time?'

Carl moved towards his father menacingly.

'Just a moment,' his father said to the phone, and put his hand over the mouthpiece.

'Carl,' he addressed his son. 'There are a few things you need to know. There is a waiting list, and also your provisional licence takes a little while to come once you have applied for it. They can't give you a lesson until you have one. The other thing is that the information the driving school is sending includes a copy of the *Highway Code*, and they want you to start studying it before you have your first lesson. There will be instructions in the pack about that.'

'Okay,' Carl replied, and dropped his arm down by his side. It was startling and quite disturbing to have his father speaking to him as if he were a person, and he felt disorientated. But at least things are going in the right direction now, he reasoned. I think I'll go to school.

He left the sitting room, returning a minute later to demand the cheque and the letter that would secure the series of lessons he so desperately needed.

Once he had these in his hand, he set off to go to school. On his way out he was sure he could hear his father's voice.

'Julia,' it said. 'It's all right. You can come out now.'

It never took long to get to school. There was the short walk to the bus stop, and there were plenty of school buses. He had put the letter to the driving school in the post box on the way. That morning, the right bus came almost straight away. He put out his arm to stop it, and got on.

Although he was a little late, he saw that there were some people from his year, so he went up to them and said, 'I'm getting driving lessons.'

They immediately looked impressed, and started asking him for more details.

'My father's paying,' he said, trying to sound as ordinary as he could. 'I'll be starting soon.'

The first subject that morning was English, which he hated; but then, he hated all the subjects, so there was nothing unusual about that. None of the subjects ever mentioned cars, so they were all useless to him.

Mr Simpson appeared, carrying a pile of jotters and a book. Carl glared at him. Mr Simpson said 'Good morning, class' in a polite voice, and put the pile on the table at the front. He went on. 'I'll just hand the jotters back quickly, then we'll get on with the class.'

Carl didn't bother opening his. He knew there would be a mass of red marks scribbled on what he wrote last week. Mr Simpson had told them to write about a book they were supposed to be reading, but it hadn't been about cars, so Carl was certainly not interested. He had only read the first page of the book, and then threw it in a bin, so he didn't know what it was about. In his jotter he had written a page about BMW cars.

Mr Simpson addressed the class. 'Since it's nearly the half-term break,' he said, 'I thought I'd read you a short story, and we can discuss it.'

Carl groaned out loud, and some of the girls scowled across in his direction, but said nothing. He could see Mr Simpson's mouth moving, but he couldn't hear anything he was saying, because by now he had switched off.

Yes, he had switched off. Over the years he had perfected an ability to do this, and it was of enormous benefit to him. When he switched off, it meant he couldn't hear a thing – nothing at all. As far as he could remember, it had first happened when he was about seven. He was trapped in a corner, and his mother was shouting at him. This was quite normal; but that time, she seemed to be shouting even more loudly than ever before.

Suddenly, something had seemed to snap inside his head, and he couldn't hear her any more. Her mouth was flapping up and down, and specks of her saliva were flying about, but there was no sound. She had hit him again, of course, and that familiar ringing sound had started up in his head, but he couldn't hear her shouting.

From that day on, he had practised switching off. At first it was a bit hit and miss; but he eventually mastered it, and for a long time he had been able to do it at will. He had had to put up with the ringing sound until he grew too tall for his mother to reach his head, so *that* had gone on for quite a bit longer.

Mr Simpson's mouth flapped around while Carl drew cars in the back of his jotter, wondering how many days it would be before the information pack containing the *Highway Code* arrived at the house. Once it arrived, he could bring it into school and study it here.

The class finished. Carl switched back on again, and could hear the scuffling noises while everyone grabbed their things and stuffed them into their bags. Then they all went down the corridor to the labs for computing. This was easier. You each had a computer and had to follow a sheet of step-by-step instructions. He usually found that he could do some of this, even if he hadn't a clue what the object of the exercise was. At least it passed some time, during which no one bothered him.

It was while he was sitting in front of the computer that he made an important decision. Tomorrow he would take the day off school. He would look up the address of ACE, and he would go there. By then they would have got his father's letter with the cheque in it, and he could get the pack from them there and then. There would be things he could find out too, like exactly when his first lesson would be.

After that he sat in a kind of reverie until it was time to go to the last class before lunch. He followed the others to another room. He couldn't remember what the class was to be about, and it didn't matter because he switched off again, thinking only of the next day – the day he would go to ACE. What a pity he had not taken a note of the address – but he could easily get it from the phone book.

When lunchtime came, he went to the canteen and took a pile of chips, which he bolted down, not noticing that he was burning his mouth.

The afternoon was games. Basketball. People liked him here. Well, they wanted him in their team. He thought it must be something to do with the fact that he could put the ball into the net. But that was easy. All he had to do was reach up, and it was in. It was quite boring really. They kept handing him the ball, and he put it in the net. It was simple.

School was over for the day, and he decided to walk home. It took a bit longer than the bus, and that meant it used up more time before he was back inside those wires again. His mother would be there, of course. His mind flashed back to how she had shut herself in the bathroom that morning. That was different from usual. He was looking forward to going to bed that night, because when he woke it would be time to go to ACE – the start of his life!

When he got in, he went straight to the phone book and looked up the address. Ah, it was in the local shopping precinct. He noticed the kitchen door was shut. He went to open it, but it was locked. That was different too. He went to his room to study magazines and car manuals that he had picked up from charity shops, and was soon lost in his own world.

Some time later, he heard his father's car, and then he heard the voices of his mother, his father and Ivy. Then all went quiet again, and he went back into his own world.

At ten o'clock, he looked at his watch. Funny, he thought. I don't think I've had any food. He got up and went into the hall. The kitchen door was open, but the light was off, and there was no one about. He switched on the light, and it was then that he saw a plate on the table, bearing a heap of sandwiches. There was a piece of paper in front of the plate, and he could see it had his name on it.

He devoured the sandwiches hungrily, and returned to his room. This had been different too; but he didn't give it any more thought, because he could get into bed now, and tomorrow he could go to the precinct and ACE.

14

4.

Carl woke early, with a sense of anticipation. He went to the bathroom, dressed himself, and then went to the kitchen. There was no more food lying about with his name on it, so he took a lump of cheese out of the fridge, and set off down the road, gnawing at it. As he walked along, he patted his pocket where he had put a slip of paper with the address on it. He didn't really need it, but it was good to have it there.

His cheese finished, he looked at his watch. Seven o'clock. ACE probably wouldn't open until nine, so he would have to find something to do to fill in the time.

He searched his mind, but came up with nothing. All he wanted to do was to go into the ACE shop. He made his way to the precinct and sat on a slatted seat that happened to be near the door he would be going through, and waited.

By the time nine came, he was quite cold. In fact, his fingers were numb. At nine five precisely, a woman came and opened the door. Fleetingly, he registered that her legs looked like everybody else's did, except Ivy's. He stood up, ready to follow her in.

'Oh, hello,' she said. 'Do come in.'

He liked that 'Do'. That's what people said to other people, but not to him. It sounded good. He didn't switch off.

'Thanks,' he said.

'What can I do for you?' she asked.

'I'm Carl Middleton.'

'Yes?' She inclined her head to one side, and looked at him with her clear eyes. He noticed how clear they were. They were not cloudy like his father's, his mother's and Ivy's used to be. Of course, they might have changed by now. He hadn't looked at them for such a long time.

'Driving lessons,' he said.

'Of course,' she answered, and took a large diary out of a drawer in a desk. 'When are you hoping for? We've got a bit of a waiting list, but we should be able to fit you in fairly soon. It will probably be in a few weeks' time.'

That fitted with what his father had said, and Carl found himself more able to speak.

'My father phoned yesterday. I posted the deposit. Now I've come to pick up the information pack because I want to get on with studying the

15

Highway Code. I want to take it to school with me.'

'The post hasn't come yet,' said the woman, 'but it should be here soon. How about having a cup of coffee?' She indicated a machine in the corner of the office.

Carl nodded. He wasn't quite sure how to respond to her, and this seemed the best thing to do.

She walked across to the machine, and collected two cups of coffee.

'Here you are,' she said, as she put one on the corner of the desk for him. 'Be careful... it's a bit hot.'

He picked it up, and his fingers began to thaw. He took a mouthful, but was as impervious to the burning sensation as he had been when he ate the chips the previous day. He noticed that the woman was holding a biscuit tin out to him, and he took three. She smiled indulgently, and he put the whole of one in his mouth, swallowing it with as little chewing as possible.

Minutes later, the postman arrived with a pile of post, which he put on the woman's desk. 'Here you are!' he said. 'A nice little heap for you.'

Carl put down his coffee, and grabbed at the letters.

'Steady...' said the woman, a little alarmed at his sudden movement. 'I'll tell you what... you look for your letter, while I check the packets.'

'Here it is!' said Carl triumphantly, and pushed it at her. 'Give me the pack now.'

'Okay,' said the woman. She opened the envelope and glanced at the letter and the cheque. 'In a rush to get to school, I expect,' she added, half to herself.

She got up and disappeared into the large cupboard at the back of the office, returning with a packet, which she handed to him.

'There's everything you need in there to start with, except the form for the provisional licence. You'll get that at the post office just along the road. I'll send a letter to you soon to confirm the course of lessons, and it'll have the date and time of the first one in it.'

Carl grabbed the pack, rushed out of the office into the precinct, and headed for the post office.

'A form,' he said to the man behind the counter.

'What for?'

Carl thumped on the glass that separated him from the man.

'Look, son, I've got a lot of forms here,' said the man. 'Tell me what you need it for, and then I can give you the right one.'

Son? His father had never called him that, he thought. Why was this stranger calling him that? Out loud he said, 'My name's Carl Middleton, and I need a form to get my provisional driving licence.'

The man pointed to the wall at the side, and Carl could see that there were a number of heaps of paper in several pigeonholes.

The man went on. 'Take one from the top heap. Those are the ones for the provisional licences. If you send the form off soon, you'll probably have it in about four weeks.'

Carl went over, took a few, and went back out into the precinct. He folded them in half and stuffed them into his information pack. School, he thought. I could go to school now I've got the stuff to study.

He arrived there at about ten, and went to find his guidance teacher, Mrs Carter. She was in her office with a pile of files on her desk. He went straight in, without knocking.

'I need help,' he said, putting his pack down in front of her.

'Would you mind sitting down for a few minutes, Carl?' she said. 'I won't be long.'

He sat down, and fiddled with the strap of his watch until she had finished.

'Right, let's have a look,' she said, picking up his pack and opening it. 'Provisional driving licence? You want a hand with the form? Yes, I can do that with you.'

She worked with him until it was complete.

'It looks as if you need to send a photo and your birth certificate too,' she said, looking at the instructions. 'Tell you what... come back to my office at lunchtime, and we can go and get a photo together. I need to renew my passport, so I need photos of that size too. You'll have to get your birth certificate from your parents.'

Carl stared at her, then picked up his things and went off to the school library. He had hardly ever been there before, but it seemed a good place to look through his pack. He put it down on a table, opened it, and spread out the contents.

He saw straight away which was the *Highway Code*. He pushed the other things back into the pack, and began to turn through the pages. Soon he was absorbed in his study of road signs and what they meant. In his imagination he was already driving along the road, interpreting the signs as he went. He scanned the pages hungrily.

Time slipped by. Carl was so engrossed in his own world that he did not even hear the bell go for lunch. It was only when he felt a tap on his shoulder, and he nearly jumped out of his seat, that he realised where he really was.

He heard Mrs Carter's voice say, 'Are you ready, Carl? Remember, we were going to get photos.'

Carefully and lovingly he slotted his *Highway Code* back into its pack, and followed Mrs Carter out of the library, down the stairs, and along the corridor to the door that exited on to the street that led to the local shops.

'There's a dry cleaner's along here that does photo processing,' said Mrs Carter. 'I saw a sign saying that they did passport photos while you wait. There aren't any photo booths locally.'

'Uh,' Carl replied, his mind on road signs and cars.

Five minutes later, Mrs Carter opened the door of the dry cleaner's, and Carl followed her in. She went to the counter and spoke to the assistant. After this she turned to Carl and said, 'That's lucky. There's a "two for the price of one" offer on at the moment. That means *you* can have your photos free!'

'Uh,' said Carl again, but then added, 'Thanks.'

He watched as the assistant stood Mrs Carter up against a curtain that was drawn across part of the wall of the shop. Was he going to shoot her? he wondered. No, he reminded himself, she was having photos taken. It was over quite quickly, and then it was his turn. He pressed himself back against the curtain, and tried to look as much like a confident car owner as possible. The flash worried him, but it did not take anything away from the fact that he knew he was one small step nearer to his objective.

A few more minutes passed while the assistant did the processing. Mrs Carter paid, and then she handed Carl his four pictures, before picking up her own and making her way out of the shop. Carl stood in the middle of the shop, staring at his image in the photos. A confident car owner stared back at him.

'Come on,' he heard Mrs Carter's voice say. 'We'd better get back now. By the way, those photos of you came out really well, didn't they?'

When they were back in school, she said, 'Come to my office for a moment, so that I can sign on the back of one of the photos for you, and fill in the section of your form that says I am the person who has signed it.'

Afterwards, Carl forgot about lunch, and went straight back to the library. All he wanted was to study his copy of the *Highway Code*. He stayed in the library all afternoon, only moving to turn the pages of his treasured possession.

At the end of the day, the librarian came to him and said, 'I'm sorry, I've got to lock up now, but perhaps I'll see you again in the morning?'

'Uh,' replied Carl, standing up from his chair. Once more he reassembled his pack, and left. Now he had a pack, the forms, *and* he had photos.

Once home, he realised how hungry he was, and it was only then that he remembered all he had eaten today was the three biscuits the woman at ACE had given him. The kitchen door was open, but there seemed to be no one about. He went in and looked in the cupboard. Good, there were some cans of beans. He opened one, took a spoon from the cutlery drawer, and devoured the beans hungrily. Then he opened another, and emptied that too. He took a few slices of bread out of the packet in the fridge, and filled a mug full of water. There was still no one about, but he decided to go to his bedroom anyway.

Having finished the bread and water, he turned once more to his study of his *Highway Code*, and immediately became engrossed in it.

Some time later he became aware of the sound of his father's car in the drive, and he looked at his watch to discover that it was seven o'clock already. He could hear voices, and could distinguish those of both his parents, together with Ivy's. He wondered why his mother and Ivy had been out so late. Seven o'clock was the usual time for his father to come home though.

The front door opened, and he could hear his father say, 'Go into the kitchen and lock the door behind you, and I'll see if he's in.'

Then he heard his father's footsteps along the hall, and there was a knock at his door. His father had never before knocked on his door. He had always just burst in whenever he wanted to; but today he knocked, and he didn't open the door.

'Carl? Are you there?' he asked, in formal tones.

At first Carl said nothing, and then he said, 'Yuh.'

'I'll see you around nine,' said his father's voice from the other side of the door.

'Yuh,' Carl replied, and returned to his studies. He could hear faint clanking noises, which he supposed were coming from the kitchen, but they rapidly faded out of his consciousness as he re-entered his own private world.

It seemed as if no time had passed before he heard his father's voice from the hall again.

'Carl. It's nine now. Would you mind coming into the sitting room?'

Would you mind? Carl repeated silently to himself. He had no memory of his father *ever* speaking to him like that. Something strange was happening, but he couldn't be bothered thinking about what it might be. All he wanted to do was study his *Highway Code.* But then he remembered he needed his father to get his birth certificate for him. Taking the form Mrs Carter had helped him to complete, he got up and made his way to the sitting room, where he found his father standing waiting for him.

'Carl,' he began.

'I need my birth certificate,' said Carl. 'I need it now. *Now!*'

His father winced as Carl's voice rose to a shout, but he controlled himself and said, 'I see you have a form there. Could I have a look at it, please?'

'*Now!* I need the certificate *now!*' shouted Carl, striding across to his father and glowering down at him. He could see his father start to shake, but gave no thought as to why that might be.

His father's voice sounded odd as he said, 'It would help us if I could see the form, Carl. Could you show me where it says about the certificate, and then I'll know what to do.'

Carl handed the form to his father, jabbing his finger at the section about what to include with it.

'Ah, yes,' said his father. 'I'll need to give you a cheque too, and we have to send a stamped addressed envelope for the return of the certificate.'

'I've got the photos,' said Carl. 'Mrs Carter went with me for them.'

'That was helpful,' said his father.

He opened the door of the large cupboard that was set into the wall, and selected a file. Soon he had the certificate, which he placed on the coffee table. Then he reached inside his pocket, took out his cheque book, wrote a cheque, and placed it next to the certificate. After that he produced two large brown envelopes, which he handed to Carl. 'One of these is for the return of the certificate, and the other is to send everything off in. I'll give you money to send this by recorded delivery, so we can be sure it gets there safely,' he said.

Carl relaxed. He didn't know why, but suddenly his father was behaving in the same kind of way as the woman at ACE, the man in the post office, and Mrs Carter at school. Tomorrow he would go to the post office and see that man again. He would fix the recorded delivery.

'I went to ACE this morning,' said Carl.

His father said nothing.

Carl continued. 'They'll send me a letter of confirmation, and they'll say when my first lesson will be.' There was a silence, and then he went on, 'I'm studying the *Highway Code*.'

'That's very good, Carl,' his father replied. 'By the way, your mother is making you some sandwiches, and she'll leave them out for you. She's going to bed early, so you won't see her. I'd like to see you again tomorrow evening at nine.'

Carl realised that he was still very hungry. He took all his things, put them in his room, and went to the kitchen, where he saw his mother working at the sink with her back to him. He could hear his father coming down the hall behind him as he said to her, 'Where's my food?'

His father rushed into the kitchen and stood between him and his mother. 'It's all right, dear,' he said to her over his shoulder, 'I'll finish the sandwiches for Carl. We've just been having an important discussion. You go on to bed now. I'll see you later.'

His mother dropped the knife she had in her hand, and scuttled out of the kitchen, still wearing an apron.

Carl sat down heavily on a chair at the kitchen table. Everything seemed different, but he was too tired to think about it. All he wanted now was some food, and then he could go to bed. Tomorrow he would go to the post office, and then to school to study the *Highway Code* once more.

His father put a plate in front of him, and began to pile food on it. First there was ham, then some salad and then some bread. After that, he produced cake from somewhere. Carl ate it all in large mouthfuls, which he barely chewed before swallowing, and he did not notice until he had finished that his father had left the kitchen.

The following morning, Carl woke early again, and was out of the house with his pack and the envelope with all the things for his application for a provisional licence, before anyone else was moving about.

He sat on the slatted seat in the precinct until the post office was open. He recognised the man behind the counter, and thrust the large envelope across to him saying, 'Recorded delivery.'

'Okay,' the man replied. He weighed it. 'That'll be one pound twenty-four pence, first class.' He put the change from Carl's pound coins back across the counter, together with the orange receipt. 'Take care of that,' he said.

Carl put it in his pack, and made his way to school and up the stairs to the library.

It was not long before Mrs Carter joined him.

'Carl,' she said. 'I know these studies are very important to you, but do you think you might be able to continue with some of your classes too?'

'No,' said Carl, and returned to his *Highway Code*.

Mrs Carter tried again. 'I've had an idea,' she said.

'What's that?' he asked.

'It will soon be the work experience week, and I've been looking around for places. Last week I came across a small garage not far away, where the owner would be willing to take someone on.'

Carl was immediately interested, and turned round on his chair to look at her.

'I thought you might like to take it up.'

'Yes. Definitely,' he replied emphatically.

'It will be in about four weeks' time,' Mrs Carter said.

Carl's mind whirled. Four weeks. By then he might have his provisional licence, and he would certainly know when his first driving lesson was to be. He heard Mrs Carter's voice. What was it she was saying?

'I'm hoping that because we've got more of the things that are important to you arranged, you will be able to go to some of your classes now.'

Carl glared at her suspiciously. Then he remembered how she had helped him get the photos yesterday, and he relaxed.

'I'll go to computing,' he said. 'And maybe to English.'

'I think you might be interested in some classes that Mr Croft is running in the lunchtimes,' said Mrs Carter.

'Why?'

'He's trying out some experimental classes in human geography.'

'Why would I want to go to that?' asked Carl.

Mrs Carter smiled. 'I think you'll find there'll be quite a bit about the structure of towns and cities, and that includes road systems, you know! Why not at least give it a try?' She stood up and left Carl staring after her.

That evening was much the same as the one before, except that Carl saw his father in the kitchen while he made food for him, and there was almost no talking. His mother and Ivy were nowhere to be seen.

After he had finished his food, and his father had disappeared, Carl went to his room. He lay awake wondering when the letter from ACE would arrive. The postman usually came before he left in the morning, as long as he did not leave early.

Carl woke very early the next morning, and lay thinking about the signs in his *Highway Code* until it was time to look out for the postman. He heard his father leave with Ivy, and he thought he heard his mother go out too, but because that was of no consequence to him he did not give it a second thought.

He was in the kitchen drinking from a carton of milk when he heard letters clattering into the hall. He dropped the carton into the sink, ran to the hall, and grabbed the letters from the floor.

Ah! Here it was... the letter from ACE. He tore open the envelope, and read the letter he found inside. His first lesson was to be on 30 March. He rushed into his room, and hastily began to write out a new calendar, one that would finish on that day. In thirty-six days' time he would be having his first lesson! He read through the letter again, and this time he noticed that the final paragraph was important. It said:

We hope you find the information pack helpful. Please study the Highway Code before your first lesson, and, if possible, obtain one or more of the books that will help you to prepare for your written test.

What were these books? He wanted to know straight away. He went to his room, got the book token Ivy had given him for his birthday, and set off once more for the precinct. At the small bookshop, he pushed the token into the hands of the surprised assistant and said, 'I want a book about the written driving test.'

'We have several here, sir. Perhaps you would like to choose,' the assistant replied politely, and he led Carl to a shelf near the till. He pointed to two books and said, 'These are the most popular.'

Carl took them from the shelf, found that the cost of both together came to fifty pence less that the value of his token, and said, 'I'll take them both. Keep the change.'

He was on his way out of the shop when the assistant called after him, 'Here's your receipt, sir.'

He grabbed it, and raced across to the bus stop, where he just managed to catch a bus to school. Once there, he went to Mrs Carter's room, and burst in to find her with a man and a woman.

'I'm sorry Carl,' she said. 'I can't see you right now. Could you go up to the library, and I'll come and get you when I'm free?'

He closed her door, and went up the stairs to the library, where he opened his new books and began to study them. He could see straight away that there were a lot of questions about the things he had been studying in his *Highway Code*. He asked the surprised librarian for some sheets of paper, and began to answer page after page of questions. He was so absorbed in his task that Mrs Carter's presence made no impact on him, even after she had spoken his name. She tried again, a little louder.

'Carl?'

He heard her this time, and stopped what he was doing.

'Can I have a look?' she asked.

'Yeah.'

Mrs Carter looked down the page of answers he had produced, and nodded approvingly. 'That's very good indeed. You have been working very hard. Now, what is it you wanted to see me about?'

'Mr Croft's lessons,' he replied. 'Where are they, and when do they start?'

'You would be best to approach him directly yourself, but as far as I know they are going to be in room 4b, and they aren't going to be at lunchtime after all. They are going to be during what would normally be your classes in modern studies.'

'Oh, I don't go to them,' said Carl abruptly.

'I know you haven't been attending those, but it doesn't mean you can't go to Mr Croft's classes.'

'I'll give it a try then,' said Carl, as he returned to his work.

At break time he went to find Mr Crofts, and learned that the classes would start the following week.

When he saw his father that evening in the kitchen, he found that there was a brown paper bag on the table with his name written on it. He tore off the wrapping, and found inside a copy of one of the books he had bought that morning.

'I've got one of these already,' he said, thrusting it to one side.

'I'll change it then,' his father replied.

'Don't bother. I've got another anyway,' he said through a mouth full of sandwich.

That night, before he went to bed, he ticked a day off his calendar. He had decided to do this each night as when he had been waiting for his birthday to come, instead of waiting until the following morning. It looked better that way.

Mr Croft's classes proved to be surprisingly interesting. Although there were many things he said that were of no interest to Carl at all, there were plenty that were. He learned about how one-way traffic systems were devised, and why. He learned about the construction of bridges, and how they were designed to cope with certain flows of traffic. He became irritable and fidgety when things like underground telephone cables and sewers were talked about, but Mr Croft soon got back to roads and cars. There was something in each lesson that was useful, and Carl took a lot of notes.

Every evening his father gave him something to eat in the kitchen. Every day at school he studied the books he had bought, together with his *Highway Code*. Every evening he studied his car magazines and manuals. Every night he crossed another day off his calendar. And twice a week he went to Mr Croft's classes. He kept on going to the computer classes, and he even went to some of his English classes.

Then the day came when the postman brought his provisional licence. It was seven days before his first lesson was due. He liked the shiny credit card style with the picture of the confident car owner staring at him from the pale green background. There were other things in the envelope too, but he didn't take any notice of them, and put them on the heap of car manuals he had in his room.

Five days later, Carl ticked off the last of the thirty-seven days, and went to sleep. Tomorrow at five, he would have his first driving lesson.

5.

The day at school seemed to drag interminably. Even his *Highway Code* and the books about the driving theory test didn't have the same pull. All he wanted was the driving lesson.

He went straight home after school, and at four thirty he was waiting at the end of the drive for the instructor to arrive. At five past five, he saw a VW Polo coming down the road with the ACE logo on it. As it drew to a halt, he could see it was a 1.4. The man who got out of it was much younger than Carl's father, but Carl did not study his appearance. All he was interested in was his lesson.

'Mr Middleton?' said the instructor, holding out his hand. 'I'm Jim Brooks of ACE.'

Carl seemed not to see the hand and said, 'What do we do first?'

'If you would like to get in the passenger seat, we can have a chat about things. I can explain the controls to you, and I'll find out from you how far you've got with your road signs and things like that.'

The time flashed past. After discovering that Carl knew the *Highway Code* from cover to cover, the instructor had introduced him to the car, but had rapidly found that he already knew much more about it than he needed for the first lesson. He had gone on to give Carl a short driving demonstration, and on a quiet stretch of road, suggested that he sat in the driving seat to try the feel of the gears and the clutch. The lesson had ended with Carl driving several hundred yards down the road, showing flawless control. How many times had he rehearsed this moment in his imagination as he studied his books and his manuals?

'See you next week then,' Mr Brooks said. 'Same time, same place.' And he drove away.

Carl sat on the slab on top of one of the low gateposts. It was six o'clock. He couldn't wait another whole week before his next chance to drive. He needed to drive *now*. His father would be home in about an hour, so he waited on the slab.

At seven o'clock, he saw his father's Mercedes slide down the road towards him, containing his father, his mother and Ivy. As it turned into the drive, he banged on the windows. His father stopped the car, got out, locked it, and addressed him.

'Don't do that, Carl,' he snapped, with an angry look on his face.

Carl grabbed him by his tie and the front of his shirt and shouted, 'Shut up! Shut up! I've got to drive. *Now!*' He towered over his father.

His face ashen, his father gasped 'Okay... *okay!* Sit there a minute while I get the others into the house.' He helped Ivy up the steps while his wife ran on ahead to unlock the door. He was soon back, and he let Carl into the passenger seat.

Still ashen-faced, he addressed his son. 'I'm afraid you can't drive this car, because your name isn't on the insurance,' he said.

'*Why not?*' Carl bellowed, angrily.

His father flinched, and cowered back into the far corner of his seat.

'Er... um.' He coughed, seemed to choke for a moment, and then gathered himself. 'I thought I'd do it once you've passed your test. It's very expensive to put a young person on the insurance of a car like this, you know.'

'I don't care!' Carl snarled. He had leaned across, and his face was almost up against his father's. 'Do it! Do it now!'

Mr Middleton got out of the car and scuttled up the steps into his house. He was gone for about fifteen minutes. When he returned, he said, 'It'll be fixed by tomorrow.'

Carl felt some of the tension in his body loosen a little. Tomorrow was one more day away. Yes, he could wait one more day, but no longer.

He turned back to his father and said emphatically, 'Tomorrow you will take me out in this car, and I will be driving it.'

Then he got out and went up the stone steps two at a time. The kitchen door was shut, and when he tried to open it, it would not budge. He went to his room and lay down on his bed. He would get some food later.

He must have fallen asleep, because it was suddenly ten o'clock, and there was no one about. He found some baked potatoes in a dish in the kitchen that had long gone cold, and he wolfed them down hungrily. Before he got into bed he had made his decision.

'I am not going to school tomorrow,' he said aloud. 'I'll wait here until I can drive the Merc.'

Carl stayed in the house all day. He could not settle to his books, and spent the day alternately pacing around, and lying on his bed.

At a quarter to seven he was on the gatepost again, waiting. When the Mercedes drew into the drive, Carl let his mother scuttle up the steps, allowed his father to help Ivy, and then he got into the driving seat. His father didn't protest, although he looked very white, and was trembling.

'Carl…' he began.

'*Shut up!*' snapped Carl, as he turned the ignition and put the car into reverse.

His father tried again. 'Can you get the L plates out of your pack?' he asked, almost pleadingly.

'Okay,' Carl replied. He put the car out of gear, and ran up the steps to the house.

Once back in the car, he threw the window stickers at his father, and put the car into reverse again. With trembling fingers, Carl's father hurriedly put them in place, while Carl carefully backed out of the drive.

He spent the following two hours driving round the local side streets. At first he drove in second gear, and then in third. His father made no comments. He was completely silent.

When they returned to the house, Carl and his father sat in the kitchen, while Carl ate most of a loaf of bread. Then Carl said, 'Same time, same place,' and went to bed.

From then on, he did not go to school. He would wait all day for his father to come home, and then he would drive for two hours. At weekends, his father took his mother and Ivy out all day, but he was back in time for the driving in the evenings.

Monday was the day for each driving lesson, and Mr Brooks would appear promptly at five. He remarked on Carl's rapid progress, but Carl never replied. He was too busy concentrating. Monday was the best day, because he drove for three hours, and he learned new things.

At the end of the second lesson, Mr Brooks had spoken to him about the written test. He had asked him a few questions, which Carl had answered accurately and without hesitation, after which he advised him to phone the DVLA and book the test. Carl had ordered his father to do it the next day, and learned that there was a place in two weeks' time. His father had tried to explain to him why that was. He had started to say that the usual wait was four weeks, but Carl had cut him short. 'Shut up!' he had said abruptly.

The day of the theory test came the day after his fourth lesson. He had to be at the centre for ten. He was up in plenty of time and caught a bus to the town to be there by nine thirty. There was a queue of people forming outside the building, and Carl stood with them until the doors opened.

Once seated with his test paper, he quickly worked through all the questions. Then he got up and left, leaving everyone else still in their seats.

The following week he received a letter to say that he had passed with full marks, and his certificate was enclosed. He didn't need that letter to know he had got full marks, because he knew that everything he had written on the paper was correct. He handed it to Mr Brooks at his next lesson.

'Great!' said Mr Brooks.

'It was easy,' said Carl.

His instructor went on. 'I think you can go ahead and book the practical test now.'

'I have,' said Carl gruffly. He had told his father to fix it as soon as he got his letter and certificate.

'What's the date and time?' asked Mr Brooks. 'I'll need to book this car for you.'

'Don't need it. I'm doing it in the Merc,' replied Carl, without looking at him. He hadn't told his father yet, but he would soon.

Mr Brooks had no doubts about this young man's level of competence as a driver. Already he drove and manoeuvred flawlessly. There were several more lessons booked, but he hardly needed them. He could just put him through everything several times more, but he was sure he would pass the test.

As if reading his thoughts, Carl said, 'I won't need the last lesson. My test is just after the ninth, and I'll definitely pass.'

'I'll see if I can fix a refund,' said Mr Brooks.

The day of the test was wet and overcast, but Carl felt exultant. Once he had passed this test, his life would begin! He had waited so long for this, and now it was nearly in his grasp.

His father had not attempted to protest when Carl told him to take a day off work on the day of the test so that he could use his car. They set off together to arrive at the test centre in plenty of time. Carl was driving of course. He could hardly wait. Nearly the last step to the start of his life! Once he had passed this test, he would tell his father which car to buy for him.

Driving with the examiner in the Merc was the best thing in his life so far, thought Carl, as he brought the car back to the test centre where his father was waiting. The examiner shook his hand warmly, and said, 'I hope you have a long and happy career in driving. That was excellent.'

Carl rarely smiled, but he beamed at the examiner, and said 'Thanks'.

As he drove away with his father, he said, 'Now we're going to the BMW garage and you're going to buy me a car.'

'But I can't afford that,' gasped his father.

'Oh yes you can,' snapped Carl. 'I've been studying your files in that cupboard in the sitting room over the last weeks, and you've got plenty of money.'

'But it's all tied up...'

'Well, untie it!'

'It'll take a while.'

'It won't stop us from ordering my car today. And take those stupid L plates off the windows.' He pressed the button that lowered the window next to him, and spat into the road as he drove along.

6.

Four weeks later, Carl was waiting outside the BMW garage to take delivery of his red convertible, with anthracite interior – a 318Ci. His father had organised payment, so all he had to do was sign something, collect the keys, and drive away. He had money in his pocket for petrol. Oh yes, he had seen to that. He wanted to drive all day, and he would need more than the few litres that were part of the deal.

He felt a sense of total euphoria as he slid out of the garage forecourt and on to the road. The sun was shining, and he had pressed the button that folded back the soft top of the car before he set off. His real life had begun. From this moment onwards he had everything he would ever need – his car... his own car. No more school, and no more prison house. The wire mesh on the windows was irrelevant now. He would sleep in his room at night of course, but he was free.

After a while, he stopped at the side of the road, took out the AA map of Britain that was in the glove compartment, and began to plan his route.

Driving along with the wind rushing through his hair, he knew he was the King. This car was better than his father's. With the top down, you had *everything.* He laughed as he realised that his father's car was actually a prison, because you couldn't fold the top back. He laughed and laughed and laughed.

'I'm better than him!' he shouted to the wind as it rushed through his hair and past his face. 'I'm better than him!' he shouted to the passers-by as he streaked past them.

Fifteen minutes later, he was on a slip road to the motorway. 'I'm better than him!' he shouted at the cars that moved to one side to let him in. His voice was snatched away by the rushing of the wind, and his ears hurt, but he didn't care. 'I'm better than him!' he shouted to the clouds. 'I'm the King!'

He pressed his foot down hard on the accelerator, and shot past the traffic in the nearside lanes. He could see flashing lights to the side and rear of his car, but he knew these were all part of the glory of his reign.

No hurry, he thought to himself. I'll coast around all day. He slowed down, and moved back across into the nearside lane.

The hours passed. The scenery passed. The clouds passed. He drove on. 'I'm better than him, I'm the King,' he said over and over to himself. It felt so good. It felt great! At last he was alive, and it felt wonderful.

He could drive all day, and sleep all night, and then drive again tomorrow. This was life... the life he had waited for, day by painful day. But now he could forget all the pain. In fact, already it seemed but a distant memory, and soon even that would be gone, now that he had his car.

Every night he returned to the house where his parents and Ivy lived, and ate all the food he could find in the kitchen. Every day he would take the money he had told his father to leave out for him, and he would set off in his car to drive until night came again.

'I'm the King, and I'm better than him,' he would shout triumphantly to the world as he drove away each morning, accelerating from standing to thirty mph as fast as he could.

Thus the days passed, and then the weeks.

It was about five weeks later that Carl began to realise that something was different. He had driven from that house in the usual way, and at the usual time, but something was different. He should be feeling wonderful, but he wasn't. Never mind, he thought. I'll get on to the motorway, and speed along with the wind in my hair. Then I'll feel great!

But after speeding along for nearly an hour, he most certainly didn't feel great, and he could have sworn he could see some wires creeping into his windscreen. He blinked several times, and they went away for a while, but they came creeping back again later.

Never mind, he told himself. There are only a few. I'll be fine. I'm the King, and I'm better than him! But he didn't feel any better.

Another hour passed, and he began to think that there were more wires. Where were they coming from? He had never seen any mention of this kind of thing in his catalogues. Perhaps he should stop and look at the manual.

He swung the car off the motorway at the next slip road, and eventually found a lay-by. Good. Now perhaps he would find an answer to the problem. He looked for wires and prisons in the index, but there was no entry for either.

Feeling perplexed, he flipped through the pages, and it was then that he noticed that the manual itself was growing wires. He felt so shocked that he threw it on to the back seat of the car, and drove off quickly, as if expecting to leave it behind.

He glanced down at his feet. Yes, his shoelaces were still tied. And he was driving a car... a car that was even better than his father's. But the wires had come. What should he do now?

He searched his mind for clues, but could find none. His father tied his shoelaces, went out of the house, and drove off. Carl knew nothing of what his father did away from the house, apart from the fact that he took Ivy somewhere. Perhaps that was a clue. Perhaps he had to put someone in his car and take them somewhere. Then perhaps there wouldn't be any wires.

By now, he was nearing what looked to be a sizeable town. He could see a school come into sight on the left of the road, and he swung his car into an empty parking place in front of the building.

As he got out and walked across towards the building, he saw a group of young people come out of a door some distance to the left of what looked like the main entrance. On further inspection, he realised that most of the group were girls, so he went across to speak to them.

'Does anyone here need to be taken home?' he asked. 'I've got room for one in my car.'

The girls started to giggle and nudge each other.

Carl repeated his question, and one of them stepped forward and said, 'Actually, it would be really helpful to get a lift today.'

He looked down at her legs. They seemed the kind that bent in the usual direction, but perhaps she would do. Perhaps he didn't need someone whose legs bent like Ivy's.

'Okay,' he said. 'My car's over here.'

He led the way to his BMW, and the girl followed close behind with the rest of her group.

'Wow!' exclaimed one boy. 'Where the heck did you get *that* from?'

'My father bought it for me,' Carl replied, as he opened the passenger door for the girl to get in.

'Crikey!' said the boy.

'Just tell me where you want to go,' said Carl to the girl as he drove out of the car park.

'Go right, and then about a mile down the road turn left. After that it's about three miles before we get to my house.'

Carl drove along saying nothing. There was nothing he wanted to say. All he wanted was to find out if this would make the wires go away. He certainly couldn't see any wires at the moment, but he felt a little cautious. After all, they hadn't been there when he first got the car, and they weren't there for several weeks; but there had been plenty there earlier today.

He heard the girl's voice. 'Can you drop me just at the end of the drive we're coming to?' it said. 'That'll be fine. Thanks very much.'

Carl let her out, and drove off. He felt a bit better. This road was very pleasant. There were fields and trees, with few houses. He began to relax a little. In fact he began to feel sleepy. Better draw into the verge and have a rest, he thought.

He woke some time later, and looked at his watch. He had given the girl a lift at about four, he remembered, and now it was nearly six. He must have been very tired. He rubbed his eyes, and it was then he realised that the windscreen was covered in wires. It was much worse than before! He felt panic rising inside him, so he turned the key in the ignition, and drove off quickly. But the wires stayed where they were. In fact, they seemed to proliferate as he drove, and the faster he drove, the faster they seemed to spread.

So it hadn't worked. Taking the girl home hadn't worked. Perhaps he should have taken her up some steps to the door? But somewhere inside himself he knew that was not the answer.

Go back and get some food, he told himself. He knew that would not change the wires on the car, but he did feel hungry, and it would be something to do while he was working out his next plan. He drew into the side of the road and took out the AA map, but when he unfolded it, it was covered with fine wire mesh, and he could hardly read it. His panic escalated.

Perhaps he could find his way by looking at road signs. Yes, that was the answer. Or he could even ask people. They might help him, like Mrs Carter or the man in the post office.

After about another five miles of driving, he was relieved to see a sign to the motorway he had left earlier in the day. He peered at it out of his side window, and found that the sign didn't have too many wires on it, so it was easy to read. Having worked out which way to go, he drove round a large roundabout until he found the entrance to the correct slip road, and soon he was driving in the right direction. Although he had slept for a long time, he still felt extremely tired. He could see enough through the wires to keep on driving, so he kept on until he was back home.

He left his car in the drive and ran up the steps, two at a time. His mother was in the kitchen, and she seemed to freeze when she saw him. He pushed past her to the fridge, took bread and milk, and staggered with them to his room. He could hear her calling to his father, but had no idea what she was saying.

He lay down on his bed, closed his eyes, and stuffed pieces of bread into his mouth from the bag he had taken. He heard his father knocking on the door and calling his name, but he did not answer. There were too many wires. They seemed to be in his mouth and in his ears. And even though his eyes were shut, he could see them everywhere.

His bread finished, he drank all the milk out of the carton, and then threw it down on the floor, where it landed on its side, and the last drops leaked out on to the carpet. But Carl didn't see this – he was overwhelmed with wires. By now he was trying to fight them off. They seemed to be wrapping themselves round him, and they were choking him.

'Aaaargh!' he shouted as he flailed his arms and pulled at his throat. 'Aaaargh!'

After that everything happened very quickly. He picked up his bedside table, and hurled it through the window. The wires must have broken, because the table landed outside. Then he ran into the sitting room and hurled books, vases, trays and small tables at the windows, which shattered and let the objects through into the garden.

'Aaaaaaargh!' he screamed. He could hear a strange sound somewhere in the rest of the house, but he wasn't interested in finding out what it was. All he was interested in was how terrible he felt.

He ran out of the front door and jumped into his car once more. Soon he was racing for the motorway. He had no plan in his mind except to drive as fast as he could – to escape.

He could see lights flashing alongside and behind him, but he took no notice, except to drive even faster.

Some miles further on he could see flashing lights ahead of him. There seemed to be a whole wall of flashing lights. For a fleeting moment he thought it must be some kind of festival to celebrate his coming. After all, he was the King... But as he approached, his subjects seemed to be all tangled up in wire, and he could not slow the car down, he was too afraid.

7.

When he came to, Carl saw that he was lying in a strange bed, in a room that was entirely white. His arms and legs hurt terribly, but he felt strangely detached from the pain. When he thought about the pain, he realised that his head hurt too, as did his chest. In fact *everything* hurt, but it didn't seem to matter.

Some people dressed in white came into the room and spoke to one another, hardly looking at him at all. He could not understand what they were saying. He could hear some sounds, but could not make any sense of them. The people went away again, and the room swam about in front of his eyes before he lost consciousness once more.

The next time he opened his eyes it was dark, apart from a dimmed light on the wall to the side of his bed. He couldn't reach it because it was too high up, and anyway he couldn't move.

He gradually realised that he was spread out like a star. He was lying on his back with his arms out to the sides. They seemed to be encased in something, and there were tubes leading from him to bottles that were floating in the air. His legs were stretched apart.

A wraith came in and looked at the bottles and the tubes. It bent over Carl's face and touched his nose. It was then that he realised there was something stuck up his nose. He tried to speak, but found he could make no sound. The wraith floated out again. It had made no sound either.

Once more his head swam, and the room faded.

The next time it was daylight, and the people were back again. He could not be sure if it was the same people, but it hardly mattered. At least it was people. He tried to speak, but again failed to make any sound. He tried to move, but his limbs felt so heavy that they must surely be tied down.

One member of the group appeared to be a woman. She glanced across at his face, and must have noticed that he was awake, because she came right up to him and said 'Hello'.

But it was too much for him. He shut his eyes, exhausted with the effort of keeping them open. He could hear the people speaking to one another as from a long distance, but again he could not make out what they were saying.

Everything faded.

Aumbries

We could see stone archways intermingled with the houses that covered the hillside, and were drawn to them. There was no signpost to follow and we had no idea what they were, so we set off walking along the most likely route.

After about ten minutes we could see a church on our right, and although there were no archways, it drew our interest. We went through the iron gates to the main door. It was locked, and I experienced a now very familiar feeling of sadness. As a child I had known churches to be places of sanctuary – the doors of which were never locked. This knowledge had meant a great deal to me. But as the years passed, many thefts and much damage had led to change, and that kernel of a sense of safety and welcome I had nursed in my heart began to shrivel. Sadness? No, it was more than that. The lurch I felt was more to do with betrayal. The places I could be sure of were no longer accessible to me. I was on the outside – excluded.

We walked on, climbing a steep side road to some new houses. Although completed and furnished, these dwellings had an air of emptiness about them, as if the lives of the owners had little or nothing to do with the buildings. We stared at a muddy field which was clearly destined to grow more sleeping units, and then turned downhill, having circled the hillside.

We were now heading back towards the centre of the village from which we had come. A gap appeared between the houses on our right, and glancing into this I saw a flight of stone steps leading up to a wrought iron gate that bore a sign. Curious, I alerted my companion and together we approached it. Through the gates we could see gravestones, and now... the arches.

Hungrily we scrutinised the words on the sign and learned that this was all that remained of a church that had been built many hundreds of years earlier. There was no indication of why it had fallen into disrepair so profound that only these arches remained. Yet there was something else too.

Several aumbries... How fascinating. Why should these have survived? I savoured the word – a word I had not read or heard for so long. It signalled something to me, but exactly what I did not know.

It was growing dark, and in unfamiliar territory it was not wise to linger. We made our way back to the stream that flowed through the village, and admired again its numerous stone footbridges.

Feeling more relaxed, we opted to extend our stay a little longer, and followed the stream to where we could see a community of low modern houses. We found a path into it and discovered that it was entirely for older people. There was no traffic, and the small units faced a central building which included an office and a large sitting room. Throughout there were many lighted windows, and we could see small groups of people sitting talking to each other with obvious ease and pleasure.

Churches. What is happening to our churches? I see regular entries in the property pages of our newspaper that list 'architect-designed church conversions'. This involves people living in a church as if it were a house. This is not a new idea, but perhaps there is more of it now. Inside are all the trappings of a house – kitchen, bathroom, sitting area, bedrooms – but would it really be a house? A church is built on ground that has been consecrated, and the church itself has been consecrated. But can what was once a spiritual home become a domestic dwelling?

Graveyards are usually protected from modern development, so why not protect our churches? A building is costly to maintain, and before it deteriorates it is valuable. If the institution of the church can no longer afford to maintain its buildings, then decisions have to be taken about their future. Is it better to convert a church into a house, or even an office block, rather than have it fall into a ruin? In purely practical terms the answer might seem to be self evident, but in terms of the original meaning and purpose of these buildings, I think it is not. In my heart I wish that any building on consecrated ground could be sold only with conditions about its use – including the lifestyle and integrity of those who might live or work there.

There is much in our modern culture that encourages the use of ancient churches and chapels as tourist attractions. In purely financial terms this may be wise, the funds so raised contributing to the maintenance of the structure and fabric of these buildings. However, it seems wrong that places of religious dedication and sanctuary should, at worst, be converted to places of tourist jargon and clatter. In those that are still used for services, visitors are requested to behave quietly and respectfully. At the very least the efforts and dedication of the many who constructed and maintained these buildings should be honoured.

I often think of how in the case of larger buildings, the years of construction span several generations of workers. In a world where we are encouraged to look for quick results, this kind of dedication and endeavour is worth considerable reflection. If the stone choir screen in Chartres Cathedral took two hundred years to carve and put in place, what exactly was the process by which this project was continued? After all, two hundred years is long beyond the lifespan of a single person.

Dates

Deceased: Return to Sender. That is what I saw on the front of the envelope. I knew instantly what this meant. This was the Christmas card I had sent to 'Uncle' Humphrey's last address. I hadn't ever sent him one before, but I had come to realise I needed to know whether or not he was still alive, and this was my way of finding out. I had chosen a card sold in aid of disabled ex-servicemen – a worthy cause. The picture on it had no link with Christmas, and I didn't like it, so it seemed ideal. Although I had included a handwritten letter with the card, I had also written my address on the back of the envelope, to maximise the likelihood of the Royal Mail returning it to me if it did not reach him. The outcome had been perfect – the card was returned to me, giving the reason. Now I no longer had to struggle with the knowledge of his continued existence, and I felt a sense of profound relief.

However, I knew very well that all was not over yet. There was much more to come. But at least I knew now that he could add nothing further to the load I had carried for so long because of his actions.

My father was a teacher of languages. When he completed his training he found a post at a grammar school. At that time Humphrey was in the sixth year of his studies, and the two gradually developed a friendship, which was terminated only by the death of my father about fifty years later. Humphrey had trained for the ministry while my father fought across Europe. My father had chosen to go – a decision my mother always resented.

I was born just after the war – in the 'bulge' year, when all the fathers were back at home. Humphrey used to come to our house when I was a baby. I am certain of this, because another friend of my parents remembers seeing him there. I have no conscious memory of these visits, but I do remember him later – coming to the house where we lived, once my father became a headmaster. Humphrey was rotund and jovial. He came to see my parents, not to see me, so I don't have any memory of conversation with him. I do have a sense that the atmosphere in the house seemed lighter when he was around, and that was always a welcome change.

When I was eleven there was some exciting news. Humphrey was now a vicar and was installed in a modern vicarage, complete with housekeeper. He had asked us to come and stay for a holiday of two weeks. A holiday... Could it really be for two whole weeks? This was amazing news!

Slowly the time passed until it was the day to get ready. There were five of us – my parents, my older brother now fourteen, and my younger brother aged four – and there was a lot to organise.

The train journey was exciting. I counted as many telegraph poles as I could, but this was a gargantuan task, and I moved on to making lists of water towers and signals instead. Big brother was a railway fanatic, and knew much more than I did, but we had a way of dividing our points of interest that avoided any friction. This was essential for survival within our family. I understand that now, although at the time I accommodated entirely unconsciously.

The vicarage was very tidy. It was warm and comfortable, with a lot of carpets. The housekeeper was highly competent – producing packed lunches and cooked meals that pleased my mother greatly. The pleasing of my mother was a central feature of my life, and it felt so good to have this burden eased, even temporarily. She exclaimed constantly about the quantity and quality of the food, and this kept her busy and calm.

The housekeeper was also very skilled with the vacuum cleaner, and she didn't complain about using it. It looked a lot larger and newer than ours. Perhaps that was the reason for her cheerful attitude to it.

The thing that fascinated me about that house was the little door that opened in the wall between the kitchen and the dining room. I had never seen one of these before, and it was a source of endless interest. I never knew exactly when it was going to open, or what would come through it when it did. Sometimes there was a face and a voice, and sometimes there was food.

Humphrey had a car, and somehow we all managed to squeeze into it. By this means many trips to sites of historical interest were possible. Ancient churches, ruined castles, Hadrian's Wall... We collected a guide booklet at each, until there was quite a stack of them. I coveted them, but I anticipated that there would be difficulty in gaining possession of any, as big brother could be a powerful adversary in such matters, and I had no way of gauging what would be the outcome.

Speeding over humpbacked bridges was one of Humphrey's delights. I loved it, and my mother protested loudly but happily at each. Good... this meant everything was going well.

The contents of the packed lunches were ingenious and varied. I remember the day when the white rolls filled with butter and dates were passed round. Mother took a bite and exclaimed with paroxysms of delight, and she continued to extol the virtues of this delicacy for many months thereafter. It is important to document that as an adult I have had a long and pernicious kind of attraction to dates, which I only began to understand when I started to remember the less pleasant aspects of our wonderful holiday with Humphrey, together with its consequences.

I should explain that my older brother was a thug. I was not able to admit this fact to myself during our childhood, and this was probably because I wasn't supposed to know. He oscillated between being helpful and being evil. One of his evil traits was in the arena of sexual torment – sexual torment of me. I now have my own views upon what had provoked him to behave in this way towards me, but they are academic. I will never know the full story unless he himself becomes conscious of it and tells me his part, and this is so highly unlikely that I can entirely discount the possibility. I will not here go into the details of what he kept doing to me when we were at home. Suffice it to say that it drove me into a frenzied state, and left me gibbering and disintegrated, with legs like jelly.

I think I must have assumed – wrongly – that while we were in the vicarage I was safe. Maybe this stemmed from my mother having told me that people could obtain sanctuary in churches. Certainly that knowledge had had a very profound effect on me, and I could understandably have extended the idea to vicarages. Or perhaps it was simply because things had always seemed better when Humphrey visited our home, and I believed that this would be the case in *his* home too. But I was wrong... very wrong.

There was a night when the thug *and* Humphrey were there, and they hurt me badly. Very badly. They had smiled in a special way as they came towards me – a way that I never saw at any other time. The mouth turns up at the corners and the face changes, but it isn't a proper smile. A proper smile is full of warmth and genuine intent, whereas this other thing is only full of self-interest, together with disregard for the fear and pain of the other.

The soft flesh of my inner arms was defiled with what came from Humphrey, and I cannot heal it. Likewise I cannot yet heal the effect of everything else that he and my brother did to me that night. I cannot bear to write it, or indeed to think of it in my conscious mind.

Since then I have never trusted men of the cloth. I have very strange feelings whenever I see one of them. For one thing, you never know what is under those robes...

I tried to tell my mother that something had happened. I can't yet remember where I was when I told her, or exactly what I said. I rather think we were in the kitchen at home. What I do know is that she nearly killed me. She struck my head so hard that I was sure she had split it open – that she had broken it and had killed me. I staggered around, and after that I remember no more... And I was condemned to eat dates instead.

I have to remember that death, so that I can find my life. I have to remember death at my mother's hands and what that meant. I remember the blow, the dizziness and staggering, the sickness, not being able to breathe... Surely this is sufficient? But no, there must be more, because there it sticks. It comes again and again in the same form, round and round in circles – the same horror, and the same death, but a *living* death. I died, but my body lived on. And now I am doomed to live out the endless repeats. But why? Why can I not move through and beyond this?

When I was a student, the thug and I went to visit Humphrey in his new post. He had long since ceased to be a vicar, and instead was working with an organisation that helped those who struggled in society. He collected donkeys, and afterwards I searched the shops to find cards with donkey pictures on them, so that I could please him by sending them.

My mother used to tell me that when I grew up the Reverend Humphrey would *'marry'* me. She told me this with a strange look in her eyes – something to do with excitement and triumph. It made me feel very uncomfortable, and I always said nothing in response. When I eventually was about to marry, she invited him to conduct part of the ceremony, but he declined, and without explanation.

In recent years my husband travelled with me to see the vicarage, and the church next to it. As I stood outside the vicarage, I *knew* without knowing. The knowledge is in my flesh and in my bones, but my head still lives in trauma and cannot know it.

The Greenhouse

The greenhouse stands at the bottom left-hand corner of our garden. Exactly how old it is no one knows. The former owners of the property told us that it was reputed to be falling down when they first arrived, but nevertheless it had survived. We took it over when we moved here twenty-five years ago, and we have propped it up ever since. The base of the greenhouse is brick up to a height of about a metre, and the glass above is framed in timber. All of it is white, but the paint is constantly peeling, and cushions of moss flourish in damp corners. Careful hands of painters and joiners have at times been employed to nurse it into continuing solidity in its extended dotage. Although its glass panes are sometimes cruelly pierced by errant golf balls from the playing field beyond, necessary replacements are always installed by us at the earliest opportunity.

Inside there are shelves and trestles of varying kinds and heights; and the undersides of all of these are adorned with swathes of cobwebs of differing age and content. The oldest are full of dirt and grime, with flakes of paint and carcasses of flies and bees. The newest are clean, and their spider owners dash across at great speed, sometimes letting themselves down on long fine threads to investigate further territory.

Every year I lift out the duckboards that cover the central area of the floor so that I can sweep out the brown leaves and other debris that have collected there. Each year these slatted boards require progressively more careful handling. The nails that hold them together work loose, and the wood itself loses substance, but careful positioning and support continue to ensure an extended life span.

On occasion a bird might fly in through the open door and fail to find its way out again, beating itself unsuccessfully against the glass. Such a situation has always worried me; but any attempts I have ever made to help these self-imprisoned creatures result in more panic and beating on the part of the sufferer, so I usually prop the door wide open and stay clear until the bird has found its own way out.

The smell in the greenhouse is wonderful. In fact, it is exquisite. As soon as I encounter it I am instantly transported in space and time to the huge mysterious greenhouses in the walled garden of the black and white mansion near where I lived as a child. On certain special days the public were allowed to make their way along the narrow walkways inside these greenhouses; and I remember the excitement I felt as I stepped down into the warm damp atmosphere and breathed in the delicious air that was trapped there. The effect it had on me was indescribable, and it has been a profound and enduring experience. Whenever I walk into my greenhouse just after spring has started to stir, or on any other day right through the growing season, I am once again the child in the greenhouses I knew long ago. The effect of the smell is as immediate and powerful each time I encounter it, and it never fails to arrest me.

At the far end of my greenhouse there is a low sink set into the ground, and just above this is an ancient tap connected to a pipe that leads from the water butt outside. It is a simple but clever device for providing a ready supply of water. Around the sink several large ferns have sprung up, and when they reach mature height, their fronds find their way through the gaps in the wide expanse of slatted staging above, and the tiny spores from the sori on the undersides appear as a brown powder on the wood. It is only with sadness and sometimes guilt that I eventually trim them down to the level of the slats. It seems so wrong to reduce them in this way, and the decision is a hard one to make. But after all, this is a greenhouse, and it is for growing edible produce – it is not a fern house. And although I can see that another fern has joined us now in the form of a spleenwort that has made its home on the wall above the sink, it is a small plant, and will never be in competition with the rest of the occupants.

There used to be a raised bed just inside, to the left of the door, but it became a breeding ground for woodlice – or slaters as they are sometimes known. These are creatures of ancient origin, and they have survived very successfully into modern times. They became adept at wreaking almost instant destruction upon anything I tried to grow in that bed, and in the end I used it only as a place to position potted plants. However, pots proved not to be the safeguard I had assumed they would be, and in the end I reluctantly authorised the removal of the slaters' kingdom. The earth and the whole of its brick retaining wall was razed to the ground, and I replaced it with three small laboratory tables, thus securing the area as one I could use without fear of further attack. The slater army is now confined to the two sacks of fibre resting on the ground, which they manage to penetrate by some means beyond my comprehension.

When early spring arrives I plant the most hardy seeds first. Once they are in pots I use the old gardener's trick of placing panes of glass on the top of each. I start with some Italian parsley – that large flat-leaved kind that grows so well and is an invaluable accompaniment to many exciting dishes. Then there is basil minette – the bush basil that likes our cooler climes.

Optimistic as always, I try beginning early with the courgette and squash seeds, and I look forward eagerly to the different coloured fruits. The large bright yellow flowers from the courgette plants are delicious. The male flowers must be picked as soon as they appear. Of course they never reach the kitchen, because they are consumed almost as soon as I gather them. There is not a shortage of eager appetites, and mine is amongst them. Not only do I prize the taste of them, but also the intense yellow colour excites me. I sometimes wonder if it draws me in the same kind of way that an insect is drawn to ultra-violet guidelines on the petals of plants such as the wood anemone, or maybe the resonance of the colour meets an inner hunger with its vibrance.

Pea seeds germinated early in the warmth are planted out to provide a ready crop. Sugar snaps are the most favoured – eaten straight from the plant. Runner beans, begun and shielded until several leaf pairs tall, have the start to enable them to dash in their spiralling gait up the bamboo wigwams that wait outside, producing their arresting red flowers along the way and ending in a mutual knot at the apex in an attempt to climb yet further. Many seeds and cuttings from vulnerable plants have been grown and strengthened here, away from competition, before being returned to their original home to try again.

Each year has brought heavy crops of tomatoes – predominantly the bush kind. The sweet bite-sized fruits suited small people very well. Their tiny hands reached out for these treasures, plucked from the drooping sheets of foliage weighed down with their trailing bounty. Sub-arctic cherry tomatoes were my favourite; but the variety I preferred became unavailable, and I missed it greatly for a long time. Cucumbers have featured from time to time, by enthusiastic request. And last year aubergine plants which I grew from seed jostled for space with the more usual occupants. Their large tomato-like flowers in purple hues fascinated me, and I felt triumphant at the sight of the fruits forming. But despite the long hot summer, the growing season did not allow these aubergines to grow much beyond five centimetres or so. I am unlikely to repeat the experiment since the plants themselves require so much room.

Apart from its plant inhabitants, the greenhouse contains various items. Until quite recently it gave shelter to a very old wooden wheelbarrow. This was an exact replica of the kind that was always used in gardens many years ago. Mr McGregor in Beatrix Potter's *The Tale of Peter Rabbit* used such a barrow, and the book includes an excellent illustration of one. However, our replica was only about a foot high, and I have clear memories of being taken for rides in it when I was very small, by my brother to whom it had belonged. I was so tiny at the time that I had to climb *up* into it, using the front wheel as a step. Sadly, the barrow became diseased: woodworm began to overwhelm it, and it was crumbling. Latterly I took several photographs of it, and finally we consigned it to the tip. In the event I discovered that I was relieved by its absence, and I can only put that down to the fact that I am also relieved by the absence of the original owner of that barrow – a brother who himself had deteriorated. An entirely different kind of rot had set in. Interestingly, the barrow had retained its original form and purpose for far longer than he had.

The small metal tricycle that had belonged to my other brother, and then to my own children, is still garaged underneath one of the tables. Its cheerful bright red paint is a reminder of good times that were never soured. Its bell is rusted and silent, but the rest of it is in good order. The sight of it brings back many happy memories of laughter – speeding along with the driver's feet whizzing round on the pedals on the front wheel, and the passenger adding velocity by using the rear bars as a kind of scooter. The handlebars had to be shared by both, but working in harmony was never a problem. First it was the golden wavy hair of my little brother that I could see underneath me as I reached my hands over to take their space on the handlebars, and then many years later the golden wavy hair was that of my own first-born son. There were times when the two almost merged into one, since for me the feelings I had in those moments were almost identical. In recent years I have sometimes used the tricycle for a slater-free pot stand, but its seat slopes backwards, and so does the plant in the pot, unless I level it with thin wedges of wood or pieces of slate.

Our garden is not very large, but it was big enough for a rectangular racetrack to be made of paving slabs round the perimeter of the lawn. In years gone by, small people on plastic vehicles dashed round and round this track, wearing out toes of shoes conveniently used as brakes. Road signs were busily produced by drawing on the slabs with chalk, and the cul-desac in front of the greenhouse door was a handy turning place. As I worked in the kitchen I could hear the rumbling of the assortment of infant tractors, cars and lorries driving past the window, and I always listened with intense fascination and unfailing interest to the cheerful chattering of their operators.

Not far from the greenhouse is a rowan tree that I grew from seed and brought with me when we came here. Its roots have now grown so big that they have displaced some slabs of the track, but this does not matter, as the child drivers deserted it long ago. The tree must be at least twenty feet tall now. In the spring its buds gradually become grey, and then they burst into leaf. The flowers follow, and in the autumn the blackbirds perform acrobatic feats amongst its branches to feast on the berries until they are no more. Year after year I abandoned any thoughts of rowan jelly in favour of allowing the birds to strip the whole crop. From my glass viewing chamber I decided that the sight of them at their labours and the gentle clucking sound they made while working was far more nourishing to me. My eyes and ears were fed by their busy movements and communication, and my mouth was happy to confine its stimulation to tasting other delicacies instead. Rowan jelly was not a necessity in my life.

The greenhouse has been mine for twenty-five years, and I have precious memories both inside and outside it. Decisions about what is grown in it are mine and mine alone. My supremacy has never been challenged. Those who benefit from the produce have always been well pleased, and I have spent contented hours playing with my pots and seeds, my mind resting and my thoughts ticking over at a gentle idling speed that allows a deeper awareness to surface. Such times are very precious. In a culture where speed and superficiality appear to be worshipped, I treasure the peace and meditative thought that the atmosphere of my greenhouse engenders. This old structure that has lasted long beyond its expected years has been a refuge for me. Its atmosphere enlivens me with a delight that touches my soul and nourishes me in times of need.

Cock o' the North

When I was a child, I had my own clockwork railway engine. It was a beautiful red colour, and it was called Cock o' the North. It had eight sections of railway to go with it, which when connected up made a complete circle. Cock o' the North had a key fixed into its side, and when I turned the key round and round, it wound up the spring that meant the engine would rush round the track. All this had come in its own cardboard box, so it was a proper set. Unfortunately, the cardboard box did not last as long as I would have liked.

I was so proud of having my own engine with its own track. This meant that I could be a person after all. My brother, who was three years older than I, had been a person for quite a long time. After all, he had a Hornby railway set.

Sometimes I was allowed to watch him playing with his set, and sometimes I was even allowed to touch it. At such times I might be allowed to help with the layout. It was so exciting! It had points and it had a turntable; it had full rails and half rails; it had straight rails and curved rails. It even had an engine shed, with big doors that opened. The engine itself was green, and, unlike Cock o' the North, was quite heavy. There were carriages for passengers, and there were goods wagons. I loved being allowed to open and shut the doors on the passenger carriages and the guard's van on the occasions when I was given special permission.

When we grew older, my brother began to build his own Hornby 00 layout. He made it on the flat wooden bit in his bedroom that was about three feet off the ground, and was the stair head. I was sometimes allowed to look at what he was doing, but I wasn't allowed to touch any of it. I was fascinated by it, because some of the parts were *so* tiny. He began by buying ready-made track, but then he progressed to constructing it himself from rails which he fixed to sleepers with minute chairs.

All these items were bought from a shop, but I had no idea where it was because I was never taken to it. In order to make some of the things he needed, he had a soldering iron. This was very important. Only important big people were allowed to have things like that. I was not to touch it of course. I was not even to go anywhere near it.

One day he let me go with him to collect pieces of gorse from a field about a mile from the house in which we lived. He had read that he could use such things as miniature trees for his layout. This meant that he would save the money he would otherwise have used to buy some from the special shop. I was so excited about being deemed to be important enough for this venture. It was a hot day, and I was wearing a short-sleeved cotton dress. I remember sweating as we walked along in the heat.

Picking the gorse was a very painful process, and carrying it was even more so. I remember my fingers were punctured in many places, and were bleeding. My legs were scratched, but apart from that they got away quite lightly.

Between us we had one large white handkerchief. We spread it out, and loaded the pieces of gorse into it. I tried to bring the corners together, but received further multiple stabs in the process. I was perplexed but undeterred. It was so important to me that I was a part of this expedition that I was more than willing to bear the pain and blood for the glory of it.

I certainly did not like the pain. Not in any way did I like the pain itself. But I liked feeling real. And being allowed to be involved in the gorse collection made me feel real. Feeling real was so important to me that I could withstand a considerable amount of discomfort and pain in order to reach that objective.

One of the things I loved to see on the stair head was the matchbox-type of containers in which certain accessories for the layout were supplied. The boxes opened to reveal minute plastic replicas of brown sacks, grey milk churns and people with clothes painted on in different colours. But I could only view them from afar. I was rarely, if ever, allowed to touch.

Many years later, I saw some in a shop. At last I could have sacks and milk churns of my 'very own', and I bought a number of golden yellow plastic straw bales as well that I saw were in the same series. I needed to own all of these. I didn't need to have a full Hornby 00 layout, but I certainly needed the sacks, the milk churns and the bales. I felt more solid as a person once I had them in my grasp. The bales had a particular significance as, not only did they belong to Hornby 00, but also my brother had never had any of them. Added to this, bales were a part of *my* life, and had never been a part of his. I could take them out and look at them and handle them. They were mine, and I was more myself.

My brother had a Meccano set. He was very clever, and he made a windmill with it. Our parents were extremely proud of him, and showed everyone they knew what he had done. They bought more Meccano for him, and he made more things that they were proud of. As his collection grew, my father converted a large wooden drawer from a chest into a storage box for my brother's Meccano. He installed several fixed wooden dividers into this drawer, the central one of which was a sliding section that could be removed if necessary. I stood and watched him making it.

I wanted some Meccano of my own, I wanted a specially partitioned drawer to put the pieces in, and I desperately wanted one of those sliding sections. Looking back on it, I know now that what I wanted most of all was the admiration and affirmation that my brother was receiving. Although my father made partitions in a drawer for me, and I was given some Meccano, the drawer was much smaller than the one my brother had, and I did not have many pieces to put in it. My father had certainly put a sliding section in the drawer, but there was a limit to the number of times I could gain satisfaction from sliding it up and down. Of course, I could always play with the handle that he had left on the front. It was one of the kind that flaps up and down, and I did enjoy putting it right up, and then flipping it down with a satisfying clunk. Of the Meccano pieces that I had, I liked the tiny nuts and bolts, together with the spanner and screwdriver that went with them. I passed some time fixing and unfixing the nuts and bolts on the girders. I liked some of the names of the pieces... 'fishplate' was one in particular that caught my imagination. But the possibility of building something was severely limited by the lack of pieces, and by a long entrenched anxiety in me about what I was 'allowed to do'. My mind simply did not function in many areas, because it wasn't 'allowed' to.

My fairy godmother came into my life when I was fourteen, in the shape of a young man. We had just moved house, and across the road was a smallholding. One day I saw that young man working there, and felt drawn to him straight away. He was standing on the cobbled yard at the front of the brick-built barn, and he was killing the weeds with a flame gun. Two years later he was 'allowing' me to do all sorts of things, including driving an old tractor. My help was useful to him, but 'being allowed' to help was *very* useful to *me*, and my severely stunted abilities were released a little. He was appreciative of most of the help I could give him, and there were many times when he would leave me with a task while he went away to advance some other project. If I got stuck, I had to use my own resourcefulness, and this was a great help to me. I reached the position where it was sufficiently developed in me for me to be able to use it to help myself in all kinds of ways; but, of course, I had to be alone. The very presence of another person would activate the question in the bedrock of my psyche of whether I was 'allowed' or not.

It is my belief that my original experiences of 'not being allowed' were ones that were accompanied by severely painful physical and emotional attacks upon me. This conditioning had certainly worked very well as far as the perpetrators were concerned. It meant that not only did I do only what I was told I could do, but also I appeared as if that was all I wanted to do – to those in charge, and to myself.

Some time after the appearance of the fairy godmother in my life, I discovered a number of very particular circumstances in which I could employ my developing resourcefulness. For example, I was having trouble in chemistry at school, and the teacher had told me unequivocally that I would fail my exams. One of the areas in which I floundered was the semi-micro analysis. I would arrive at the lab at the appointed time with the rest of my class. We would put on our lab coats, and get to work. I loved the apparatus. Everything was about half the size of the equipment we had always used before – a dear little Bunsen burner, together with its small tripod and matching tiny test tubes. All these were a delight to me, and lifted my heart. But there were insurmountable problems. The rest of the class had no difficulty in seizing the apparatus they required, while I hung back, and waited... until there was little or none left. The next pitfall was the book of instructions. When I tried to read it, it swam before my eyes, and I could make very little sense of it. Then the teacher would come and shout at me, further adding to my fear, confusion and distress. Of course, I never finished in time, a fact that led to further vilification of me.

I don't know how the idea first came into my mind, but one day I decided to go to the lab early. This session was straight after the lunch break, so there was plenty of time. As soon as I had eaten, I went there, put on my overall, and made a start on my work. In the absence of the rest of the class, obtaining the necessary apparatus was not a problem, and I soon had it assembled. Then I set about the task of studying the instructions in the book. Each week we were given an unnamed compound to analyse, and this book supposedly told me how to go about it. This time, to my surprise, it all seemed quite simple and straightforward. Why was it that it had all appeared to be gibberish before? I could only assume that this had something to do with the presence of the rest of the class, and possibly the teacher herself. That day, I completed the assignment for the first time – and I completed it long before the session ended. The brighter pupils, who had arrived twenty minutes later than I, were still working long after I had finished. In fact, most of them finished the task well over twenty minutes later, so proving to me that not only could I do the work, but also I could do it quickly and efficiently. From that time on, I made sure I went straight to the lab to get a head's start, and I had no further problems there. When it came to the practical exam, although I had to start at the same time as the others, the equipment had already been shared out fairly, and I had retained the confidence that I had built up over the weeks. I sailed through that exam without any difficulty.

Of course, when I was younger, my brother had made a chemistry set for himself. He had it in the garage that stood next to our house. We didn't have a car, so the garage was used for making things in, and for storage. He had his own wooden workbench under the window that let in daylight, and he had a book that he kept somewhere in his room that explained what to do. I remember I was sometimes allowed to watch him when he was doing his experiments, but of course I already knew that I mustn't touch any of his things. He had made a burner out of an old metal container. I think it had once had Brasso in it, but the contents had been used up long ago. He had cleaned it out, and made a hole in the lid. He filled it with cotton wool, and then added methylated spirit. With a piece of the soaked cotton wool protruding through the hole, there was something to light to make a burner. He went to the chemist's shop, and returned with little packets of interesting-looking crystals. I was allowed to have a few out of one of the packets, and he even let me taste the colourless crystals of citric acid.

When I was a child, we weren't allowed to read *Beano* or *Dandy*, except when we were away on holiday. When we were at home, my brother had *Eagle*, and I had *Robin*, although as I grew older I graduated to *Swift*. *Robin* was all right for a while, but after that I found it uninteresting, and *Swift* was never any use to me. On the other hand, the Eagle was very interesting indeed. The Mekon was a character of enormous significance, second only to the Treens. Fortunately for me, my brother let me read all the issues of *Eagle* that he received, so long as I waited until he had read them first. He also had an *Eagle Annual* each Christmas, and he kindly let me read these when I was ill in bed. They were certainly worth reading. And in the weekly issues, 'See next week's exciting instalment', 'To be continued' and 'To be concluded', were phrases that left me in a rather more intense emotional state than mere eager anticipation.

I would have liked to own some of those *Eagle Annuals* myself, but the level of deprivation I suffered through this lack of possession was not all that great. However, there was certainly a problem about the *Rupert Annuals*. There were very few of these – perhaps only two or three – and again, they all belonged to my brother. For some reason, the Bird King inspired in me a sense of such wonder and delight that I felt completely transported to another state of existence. And my brother owned the portal to this state – the annuals.

About fifty years later, I discovered that there were many collectors of *Rupert Annuals,* and that there were old copies for sale. I bought a copy of the *Rupert Index*, and hungrily scanned its pages for the titles of the tales that appeared in each annual. Excitedly, I ordered the one I hoped I needed. The lurch of feeling that I experienced as I opened the packet which subsequently arrived could only be that of the small child whose very existence had depended upon the ownership of such a volume. I felt the expression on my face transform to a beatific glow as I cradled the treasured book in my arms and then clutched it to my chest. I believe that for that moment I experienced a feeling of complete and utter fulfilment.

North Park Road was the road that led to the rear entrance of the primary school I attended. It branched off from the north side of Park Road, the road where we lived at the time. Our house was on the south side of the road. The front faced north, and the back faced south. That meant that the front was the cool, dark side of the house, and the back was the sunny side.

My brother had a compass, and seemed to be able to use it. Without a compass I kept getting west and east muddled up, but apart from that, I managed to get a mental picture of how such directions as north-west and south-east came about.

It is my life's work to continue to seek my own bearings, and to enable others to do likewise.

Fried Onions

She handed the little black and white photograph across to me, and I stared at the small stone dwelling on a distant hill. So this is where my friend had lived with her shepherd husband all her married life.

'I can't see the road that leads to it,' I commented.

'There isn't one.'

I digested this piece of information. No road, and no other buildings in sight: an isolated life indeed. I sensed she was disinclined to say more, and we returned to our task of amusing my infant son, who was sitting on my knee.

My friend had begun her working life 'below stairs', and her kindly mistress had been concerned enough to buy for her a set of false teeth, as she had lost all but one tooth due to lack of care. I learned that she had kept the teeth but had never worn them. Her one tooth had stood the test of time, and was clearly visible at the right of her lower jaw.

'There's a little mouse in the cupboard!' she squeaked, and my son smiled and giggled in response. He loved this simple game.

After a while she fell quiet, and I noticed that she looked tearful. I waited, trying to appear as if I hadn't noticed, as I sensed she might not want to admit to her distress.

At length she said, 'My husband loved fried onions, but I didn't like them at all.' She paused before confiding, 'I wish I had cooked them for him. I feel so guilty that I didn't.' She started to cry.

I could do nothing for her but wait patiently while she felt again the pain of her husband's absence. As far as I understood he had been dead for twenty years or more.

My friend lived in a small ground floor flat. The wooden porch was big enough for my pram. The narrow hallway led to the living room on the right, and at the end was a small bathroom. I never saw the kitchen, but I think it was the corner of the living room that was hidden behind a screen. I often noticed the smell of boiled cabbage as we sat and passed an hour together.

I had first met Mrs W through our health visitor. It was during the first winter of my second son's life that I began to consider how lonely housebound people must feel, and I had made enquiries about older people in the locality. At first the health visitor's response was discouraging, but then she thought of Mrs W and arranged for me to call round. Our friendship blossomed almost straight away, and I would sit with her for an hour every week, latterly taking with me one or two slices of cooked ham – her favourite.

Mrs W was in many ways a very private person, but she was generous with her warmth towards me and my son whenever I called. However, as time went on I noticed a change in her. She began to comment on the fact that her home help came only on weekdays, and I felt that she was becoming frightened about being alone at weekends. It was difficult to know what to do. Our relationship had never extended to one where her care was discussed, and this was how she had wanted it. There is a delicate balance between appropriate concern and intrusion, and I was not sure where this boundary lay. Sometimes I would make the slice of ham an excuse to put my head round the door on a Saturday, but I did not feel confident about my approach.

Feeling anxious one Monday morning I went to see her quite early, and found the house full of people. They told me that they were relatives, that she had died over the weekend, and that I could not see her.

I was very distressed. A few days later I sat through the small funeral, and I attended the burial ceremony. All the time my head filled with everything I must remember to tell her when I next saw her – the behaviour of her relatives, what the minister had said...

I was distraught. Perhaps I should have been less cautious about risking appearing intrusive in her life. To me, she had died not only alone but also frightened. I searched my mind. What else could I have done for her? Blindly I sought comfort in the arms of my husband, and at that point our daughter was conceived – unplanned and unexpected: a gift.

Do you believe in reincarnation? Do I?

It is my belief that no one should die alone, but I have to accept that many do.

Fried onions – a symbol of regret for what could have been but never was, and a focus for sadness when acknowledging one's side of that story.

We all have our fried onions, whether or not there is a death. Could I have helped my friend more? There is no way of telling. At the very least, surely I have learned from the experience of losing her as I did? But twenty-five years on, I am not sure that I would have done anything differently. I was her welcome visitor, and represented the part of her week in which she could be herself in a very particular way. Others in her life – the health visitor, the home help, the neighbours, and even the absent relatives – were those who monitored her daily needs.

But the kernel of doubt lingers on in my mind, and I think about what I learned about my friend and about myself when I think of others who may be about to leave us.

The Psychiatrist

I opened the corrugated paper parcel. *Talking about Psychiatry* the spine of the book inside informed me. With some trepidation I searched the index and located a page. The man in the photograph stared at me. I felt sick. I wanted to scream, but no sound came. I wanted to run away, but there was nowhere to hide, and in any case my legs could not carry me. I turned the page and became dimly aware that this was the account of an interview with him. I saw the words 'What did you do when you were in Bromcaster?' and blackness descended. When I came to, I was small again.

*   *   *

The kitchen was at the back of the house. It had a large – almost bay – window, and when the sun shone it could be quite warm. The Creda cooker stood to the right of that window. Then there was a kitchen cabinet: it had doors at the top that opened to reveal shelves for dry goods, a door in the middle that swung down to form a work surface, and a further cupboard at the bottom. To the left of the window was a corner cupboard full of plates and dishes. I collected the dark blue labels from bunches of bananas, and was allowed to stick them on the front of this cupboard. My favourite one bore the word 'Fyffes' and then, in smaller writing, 'Fernando Po'. The triangular labels from Swiss Knight cheese had joined the banana label collection.

The fireplace was on what should have been an outer wall, but on the other side was a lean-to, which housed the newly-installed toilet, and the wash-house. The wash-house was used only on a Monday, and then it was used *all day.* There were duck boards to avoid getting wet feet. Apart from the large, deep sink directly under the window, there was a boiler, and a dolly tub which stood underneath a mangle. The old mangle had been replaced by the Acme Wringer, with its adjustable rollers. The sheets purred through it, emerging much less wet. The boiler had a long truncheon-shaped baton standing beside it. This was for prodding and probing the clothes. But there was also a fascinating implement on the end of a pole. This was called the 'posser' – like a model of a Martian space ship, with its bell shape and the holes around it.

The 'back' door of the house was really at the side. A door at the left of the fireplace led from the kitchen into a small lobby where there were two doors. One was the outer door, and one was the door to the 'cellar' – a small pantry, half below ground. The lower end of this housed a slab on which food could be left to keep cool. There were earthenware crocks for storing bread and flour, and there were shelves for jams. Lengths of seaweed hung below the shelves to help us to determine the weather. I once saw a mouse running across the floor of the cellar – but Mother firmly told me that I had not.

In the wall opposite the window of the kitchen was a recess, which we called the Pantry. Here was a sink under an internal window that looked into the lobby, and there were many cupboards, low and high.

There was a drop-leafed oak table at the window with several chairs, none of which matched, and this was where we normally ate. From my chair I could see out into the garden; but as the window sill was relatively high, I could not see anything but the tops of hedges, bushes and trees, together with the upper end of the iron-framed swing.

Our house was semi-detached, but the rest of the houses on that long, tree-lined road were detached, and were *very large*. Some had *enormous* gardens that backed on to the Park, which was the extensive grounds of a very old mansion house.

At the other side of our neighbours' house was a cinder track, followed by a very large house, and then another. In that second very large house lived a boy of about my age. How I met him I do not know. He was wild and unpredictable, and when with him playing was almost impossible. I don't ever remember his being in our house. I remember being in his garden, where he danced on top of the compost heap and scratched my face with a stick – an event which incensed my mother, who dragged me back along the road to show the damage to his parents.

I also remember being in his house, although only rarely. There I was always part of a group, and invariably I felt small and at a disadvantage. The house had a curious feature – there was a small room directly above the front door, and the window that lit this room looked out above that door. The entrance to it was by way of a small door in one of the bedrooms to the front of the house. This door was made of wooden boarding, and was hinged on the left. A special door, and a secret room... Since the room itself was below the level of the first floor, there was a drop into it, and this is what I did not like. I was small, and not very agile. If I got down into that room, how would I get back out again? I was dependent upon the help of others to climb out. I wanted to be a part of it all and I wanted to join the others, but could I trust them to help me out again? Each time I went in, there was always an anxiety in me.

The boy's parents did not seem to be interested in what we were doing, so long as we were quiet. They were distant figures, hardly seen. But one day was different...

It was the beginning of summer, and the huge horse-chestnut trees that lined either side of our road were in full leaf. The striking white flower spikes – which we always referred to as 'candles' – were over for the year. There was a sense of change in the air. Being young, I could not name this, but I knew it.

There were many people visiting that boy's house, and I was allowed to go and play. In fact, I was *encouraged* to go. Feeling quite important, I walked along the path to the house, and up the drive. There was a hum of voices, and the house was full of big smiling people, carrying glasses and talking. People whom I thought were the boy's parents smiled at me and said 'hello'.

As always, the boy had several children with him. I was never very sure if any of them were his brothers or sisters. I later found out that two were his older sisters. As before, we went upstairs, and as before, we opened the special door into the secret room. I could hear the noise and bustle and laughter from below, as once more we jumped down into that room. The big people were busy with their important lives: the children were fine to have around so long as they did not bother them. I did not feel relaxed here: I never did. I never really felt part of it; but I was always intrigued by this room, and today I felt different because I had been invited to come, and the people downstairs seemed to be very important.

But something went wrong. Something went *very* wrong. I do not know what happened, but whatever happened was *very* wrong.

The other children were giggling and silly that day, and the thing I had always feared happened. They left me in that room – trapped. They laughed at me when I could not climb out, and then they ran away. I was frightened and horrified. What should I do? There was nothing I could stand on to help me to climb out. I felt lumpy and useless.

I do not know how much time passed. I could hear clinking and laughing noises, and sometimes music and songs rising up from downstairs as I crouched, miserable, in my prison. It was not really a prison because the door was open, but I could certainly not escape. I felt exhausted, and despairing.

It was then that I heard footsteps, and they came into the bedroom above me. I felt my body tense with expectation, but I uttered no sound. A face peered through the small door and smiled at me. It was a man's face – *that* man's face. He looked amused when he realised my predicament, but he reached out a hand to help me up out of my prison.

Standing in the bedroom with him, I did not know what to do or say. This was a situation that was entirely outside my former experience. I was standing in a bedroom with a strange man who had just rescued me from a prison. He was wearing a three-piece suit, and he smiled at me. I was numb. If I had not been numb I would have been crying because I felt so miserable. I felt miserable about what the children had done to me, and now I seemed to be frozen.

I glanced up at the man's face again, and his smile broadened. I quickly diverted my gaze back to my shoes. I felt *very* uncomfortable. Why was he smiling like that? It did not look right, and it did not feel right. A hazy realisation began to form in my mind that this was the boy's father.

My mother was a person who believed that children should only do as they were told. Having been thoroughly trained in this discipline, I waited to be told what to do. Although I felt numb, I also felt slightly sick, and I struggled inwardly to conceal it.

The man put out that hand once more – his right hand – this time clasping my upper arm. My sense of it alerted me to the fact that this was no ordinary touch. It was not there to reassure me that everything was all right. It was there for some other reason, and I did not know what that was. All I could do was wait to be 'told'.

I gazed fixedly at my shoes, and my body stiffened while his other hand took my other arm, his grip tightened, and I found myself being lifted on to one of the two single beds. By this time he was speaking, but the words made no sense to me. Some I recognised, but as they were strung together in a way that made no sense, I could not make any use of them.

His breath smelled funny, and I did not like it. He pushed my stiff sitting shape flat on to the bed, and obediently I took up that position. Now I could see his fingers fumbling with the fastening of the trousers of his suit. What was he doing? I knew from the fastening of my brother's short trousers that there would be buttons hidden there, but what was he doing with them?

I lay in my stiff flat shape, and stared as he fumbled. His words changed to grunts and groans, and I began to think he might be ill. What should I do? Should I get help? But I could do nothing because this man had made it clear to me that I had to lie flat on my back on this bed. All I could do was wait for his next instruction.

What could this be? A mountain of flesh appeared out of his trousers. He must be very ill indeed. How could his body produce this mountain without there being something terribly wrong? He seemed to be panting, but it was not the kind of tired panting our dog did when she was hot or thirsty – it was an urgent, desperate panting.

He pulled up my dress. Why? My mother pulled up my dress when she was helping me to take it off, but I would not be lying on a bed at the time, I would be standing up. He pulled my underwear down. I was so frightened I wanted to scream, but I could not. My mouth was clamped shut, and I could barely breathe. His body came over me, and I felt intense pain in my whole being.

The man said a very bad word, a word my mother had told me I must *never* use, although I had heard *her* use it once, when she had knocked something over that might have broken. He pulled himself upright and then grasped my mouth and forced it open. Leaning across my face with his flesh mountain he pushed it hard into my mouth. Choking, I tried not to gag. *I must not.* My mother hated vomit, and she might hit me. I could feel wetness run down on to my neck, and I tasted salt in my mouth.

The man's body had sagged. He had rolled off me and was kneeling on the floor, leaning on to the bed.

'Get up' he hissed at me. 'Get up... *now.*'

His voice conveyed a sense of great urgency, and I did as I was told. He pulled a handkerchief out of his pocket, wiped my face and my neck, and rearranged my clothing. I could hear voices downstairs calling a name. Was it *his* name?

I could hear 'Time for the cake. Come on ... where are you? We've lit the candles.'

There was no sign of his flesh mountain, and his fastenings were in place. Where was it? Had I imagined it? How could anything so big have disappeared without trace? And he was speaking now in a way that I recognised.

'Come downstairs with me,' he said.

He took my hand and led me down the stairs.

'Oh *there* you are,' I heard several voices saying.

'Sorry about the delay,' he replied. 'I found Mary in the lumber room upstairs. She was too small to get out by herself, and the others had left her there. I must speak to them.' He turned to me. 'Now run on back home dear, I expect your mother will be waiting for you. The others went home half an hour ago.'

One of the people led me to the front door, and I followed obediently. I was so shocked I could hardly see. I heard a voice say, 'She looked a bit pale, I expect she got quite a fright.' The man replied, 'Yes, a little thing like that, alone in the lumber room. I must have a word with her mother to tell her exactly what happened, because I think Mary might be a bit confused about it.' The door closed behind me and I made my way slowly down the road to the house where I lived.

'Where on earth have you been?' snapped my mother as I went through the side door and into the kitchen. 'I told you to be home by six at the latest, and it's well after that.' She scowled at me.

Oh no... I had not done as I was told, and I was likely to be punished for it.

'*And* you've got some mess on your dress. Look!' she said accusingly, as she pointed to the neck of my dress. 'What on earth have you been doing?'

'I got shut in,' I said miserably, not expecting to be believed.

The phone rang, and she went to the hall to answer it. I could hear her speaking to someone, but I could not make out anything she said, as she had shut the door. When she came back she was not so angry.

'All right,' she said. 'They just phoned me. I expect you were crying and dribbling, and that's why you've got this mess on your dress.'

I began to think I would not be punished after all.

'I hope you weren't sick!' she added irritably.

I shook my head mutely.

'I'll wash your dress tomorrow,' she said.

I could not eat my tea. I expected trouble, but she was sympathetic.

'I expect you're too upset to eat after being shut in like that. You can catch up in the morning.'

I was profoundly grateful, and even more so when she suggested I went to bed early. I went upstairs and took off the dress. I washed my face and my neck as best I could. There was a slightly odd smell, and it reminded me of fish.

I lay in my bed, with the pale green chintz curtains drawn together across the window. I counted the clusters of coloured flowers that were printed on them, I counted the stars on the pattern on the ceiling paper and I stared at my pale green plastic shoulder bag that was hanging off one of the knobs on my dressing table. It had a small side-pocket on it in the shape of a heart.

*　　*　　*

The book was shut on the floor in front of me. I stared at it stupidly.

I knew very well what he had done when he was in Bromcaster. It was no secret to me now.

Part II

Sexual abuse of children

[For 'he' (the child), read 'he or she'; for 'him', read 'him or her'; and for 'his', read 'his or hers'.]

How would you feel about your house being burgled – your possessions smashed, tainted, sullied or removed? Think about it. Imagine it. Coming home to the place where you want to feel secure...

How would you feel about your body being burgled? Penetrative sexual abuse is precisely that – it is the burgling of a person. It is the burgling of a body and a soul. The abuser breaks into the body, treating it like trash. How can that be cleaned up, repaired, put to rights?

Bad enough to have the inside of a building defiled, but unlike the body and soul of a victim of sexual abuse, it can be restored relatively easily. A person carries his body with him wherever he goes. He who has been abused has to carry that with him. He cannot leave behind the defiled place. It is therefore not surprising that suicide or other self-harm is not uncommon in sufferers of sexual abuse. Depressive states abound.

The child depends upon adult people for a blueprint of proper, loving behaviour. The child needs adult people to respond to him in a way that shows him who he truly is as a person. The child needs a context in which he can discover his own sexual feelings, secure in the knowledge that adult people will help him to understand and value these feelings so that they become an integrated part of his personality, a part of him that he can later choose to share in a committed relationship with a chosen partner.

If instead the child becomes the object of focus for the sexual dysfunction and sexual distress of a person who is older and larger than he, what then? What happens to this child? His sexual feelings are not discovered by him in his own time and in his own way – they are forced into being. The child is robbed of his own sexual dawning.

How can someone ever do that to a child? It is the ultimate betrayal. Behaviour and actions which belong only to the trusting intimacy between people become the basis of a crime of violence. It is the ultimate distortion – delivered by a 'smiling' torturer.

The physical actions that lead to the abuse are varied. The emotional play with which the abuser wields power over the child is also varied.

The term 'penetrative sexual abuse' is usually applied to a finger, a penis, or a penis-like object, being inserted into a body orifice against the will of the abused. The body orifices usually involved are the mouth, the anus and the vagina. However, ears are also orifices, and can also be violently entered.

It is important to recognise that verbal sexual abuse can be experienced by the abused person as an aggressive penetration. More subtle use of verbal sexual abuse can distort the child's reality, drawing him into distortion, not dialogue. Severe sexual abuse can be inflicted entirely by verbal means, since a physical and emotional response can be obtained solely by employing this route.

It is sexually abusive to require, coerce or otherwise force a person to touch or rub the sexual parts of another.

It is sexually abusive to coerce a child into removing his clothes in order to photograph his nakedness to elicit sexual stimulation in another. The child will have a sense that it is not right, although he may not be able to articulate this, or demonstrate his unease.

Abusers may 'reassure' children that what they are suggesting is all right, e.g. 'your mother liked this too'; 'this is what big girls do'. They may say things to frighten the child into complying. They may concentrate solely on using their superior strength.

The word 'paedophile' is of Greek origin and means 'child lover'. A person so named in our society is no lover of children. He or she is a

67

person who has little or no regard for the feelings and situation of the child, and is focussing primarily on what he or she experiences as personal satisfaction or gain.

Love is essentially a state in which there is mutual rightness and trust. The abuser may have intense feelings or impulses which are focussed upon the abused child, but this is *not* love.

Giving love to a child is a process that fills the child with the knowledge and value of himself. This cannot ever be achieved by filling the child up with foreign body parts or objects, nor with words designed to manipulate and engage the child in verbal interplay for the sexual arousal of the abuser.

In the context of medical examinations and treatments it is important for the practitioner to remember to ask the patient for permission to examine him. This is always important; but it is of even greater importance if the patient is someone who has been abused.

About abusers

There are those who are so focussed upon the objective of obtaining for themselves the intense sensations associated with sexual arousal and activity that they are oblivious of the suffering of the small person who is having this behaviour imposed upon him. Their self-gratification is paramount. Such abusers may be totally unaware of the fact that they are indeed abusers.

There are those who sexually abuse children with the express intention of causing hurt and harm, who enjoy inflicting that hurt and observing the physical and emotional pain of the abused.

Of the people who themselves have been sexually abused in childhood, there are those who have not faced the harm it caused them, and can unconsciously assume that because they were treated like that, this is a normal way to behave.

There are abusers who try to justify their behaviour by saying, 'But I could see him/her responding'. It is very important to remember that the human body is made in such a way as to experience pleasure sensations in response to sexual arousal. This can be true *even in cases where the arousal is the result of forcing by an abuser*. Even where a child is fearful of a situation and clearly disliking it, he can exhibit a visible physical arousal response. A child should never be exposed to such a situation. Adult survivors of child sexual abuse often report feelings of guilt about having experienced sensations of arousal, and helpers must take this into account.

'Flashers'

It is often assumed that a man who exposes his erect penis in a public place does so solely to observe a reaction of shock in the person(s) forced to observe it. I believe that this is not always the case. Such people may be 'boys in men's clothing', boys who in their childhood needed to hear discussion of sex and sexuality, but heard none. In such cases the 'flashing' can be the person's only concept, however inappropriate, of initiating a discussion about sex.

Some comments on the legal situation

As I understand it, current law uses as its base written and spoken records of events. In a case where a child had been sexually abused, the record would state, for example, how a man or woman approached a child and what that man or woman did and said. The record would include the child's memory of this, and any signs of damage to the child's body which have been noted by a medical practitioner. The precise emotional states evoked in the child are not identified and included. The emotional and psychological distortion and damage inflicted upon the child are not identified and reported.

In a well-publicised High Court case, the abused brother of an eleven year old girl, who had also been abused, was asked the question, 'What did your father do to you?' His answer was very clear. He showed the Court a large part of *exactly* what his father had done to him – by *expressing the emotional reaction* which had been evoked by his father's behaviour towards him. The anguish and distress he suffered were clearly audible and visible. He was completely unable to communicate with words. I would guess that his father had never asked his son, 'What have I done to you?' The Prosecutor had raised the question, and the boy had answered in the only way he could. Yet the law as it stands does not deem that to be any answer at all. The case collapsed. It was feared that the boy would be 'psychologically damaged' by further questioning. Yet the boy had already been psychologically damaged and was *showing* his distress to the people who professed to want to know about it. Limitation and reduction of psychological damage can be achieved if the sufferer is allowed to express his distress and is accepted and received in it. This is a particularly important principle to bear in mind for those who wish to review all aspects and levels of the way in which cases of child sexual abuse are dealt with.

Incidence of child sexual abuse

When considering this question it is essential to have a clear description of how any statistics are obtained. Even in cases which have come to the attention of the authorities and are therefore documented, we cannot be sure of the extent of the abuse. It is my view that it is commonplace for child sexual abuse not to be reported. A child who is being abused in his own home is very likely to be unable to speak about it until he is no longer living there. Even then, the inner conflicts and painful emotional states that such a person has to dwell in often mean that the abuse is not spoken about.

The trauma of sexual abuse in childhood is one which can be repressed by the child. In my counselling practice I have found that over 50% of my clients have suffered some form of sexual abuse in childhood. Of these, there are those who show clear or peripheral symptoms of having been abused but have no conscious awareness of the abuse itself. In such cases it is extremely important to allow the client to 'rediscover' the abuse in their own way and in their own time. In these cases it is likely that the client will start to remember some of the context of the abuse before remembering the abuse itself. If so, the client has constructed the stage on which the events themselves can be remembered, with confidence about their authenticity. It is essential to recognise this.

Parents

A parent may be an abuser or may be someone who fails to notice that their child is being abused. A parent may *choose* not to notice that their child is being abused, or may notice but fail to protect the child. A parent may even be pleased that the child is being sexually abused. For example, a woman may be glad (for a number of reasons) that her husband is 'satisfying' himself by abusing their son or daughter.

A child may attempt to tell a parent of the abuse that he is suffering. In such a case, the child may well not have the vocabulary and understanding with which to articulate clearly what is happening to him. For example, 'Daddy put a needle in my bottom', when taken literally, can be viewed as being very unlikely. However, if one thinks of the kind of pain produced by attempted penetration of a small orifice, this may well be described best by a child as a 'needle', if the pain of being pierced by a needle is the nearest comparable pain to that which he is experiencing. Young girls may refer to either their vagina or their anus as 'bottom', although later they may use the terms 'front bottom' and 'back bottom'. Without the aid of a mirror a girl cannot usually see her genitals, and it is therefore more difficult for her to grasp what is there – unlike a boy's genitals, which are very apparent.

Thus the parent may not understand what the child is trying to express.

A parent may grasp what the child is trying to say but may disbelieve the child. Such disbelief might be naïve, e.g. '… but you are too small for him to have done that'. Or there may be an aggressive attempt to destroy the child's reality for some spurious reason, e.g. 'You bad girl, you are lying, you are making it up, you are just trying to cause trouble. It is evil to say that Uncle …. did that. Don't you dare make up anything like that again.'

The introduction of sex education into primary schools has meant that more children learn the language with which to describe sexual events. However, the education programme is not usually introduced until the later primary classes. Some schools have used the programme based on extensive, successful Canadian work. To begin with, the children are encouraged to develop a clear view of their own personal boundaries, and to apply the 'feeling yes, feeling no' test to situations. The child can therefore develop a more conscious awareness of feelings of intrusion. Later in the teaching programme children are actively involved in considering alternative options if they cannot find someone who will listen to their worries about sexual matters, and they are encouraged to keep trying by approaching parents, neighbours, or teachers. Such education is invaluable. Television can have an important role. I knew someone who realised that the abuse that she was suffering in her home was wrong because she saw families on the television where such things did not happen.

Trauma of entry

When being entered via the vagina or anus, the child will experience intense physical pain.

When a penis is inserted into a child's throat the airway is obstructed, and if this continues the child will enter a death experience. Such experience is clearly documented in Gita Sereny's book about Mary Bell (*Cries Unheard: Why Children Kill: The Story of Mary Bell*).

Ejaculate in a child's throat can cause a sense of choking/drowning.

Stark realities

Rape is not only a crime against the raped person, it is also a crime against humanity as it carries with it the possibility of creating a human being who is born out of torture.

It should be remembered that the age at which a girl begins menstruating is lower now than it was a generation ago. It is not uncommon for a pregnancy test to be performed on girls as young as nine years old who are being examined for abdominal pain.

Sexual abuse affects the whole life of the child – for ever. If the sufferer has a chance to remember and review what happened, now in safe secure interaction, there is the possibility of consigning abusive experiences to the past, rather than having them live on, trapped inside, causing perpetual pain.

Recovered memories

(i) True or false?

I have both a personal and a professional involvement in developing a sense for the accuracy and authenticity of material presented in cases where a person is recovering memories which have previously been repressed. It is of paramount importance to me that my professional involvement with people who are 'recovering memories' is always meticulous with regard to the examination and understanding of what the client is trying to tell me – in words, actions and appearance.

In my practice it is usually the case that people may start to think of things which they have not thought of for many years, but which they have never forgotten, and so had never been repressed. Such things, when thought of again, are available to be looked at, perhaps in new ways. Interested and informed questioning can lead to the client confiding more and more. Thus, in the therapeutic setting a picture is gradually built up of clients and their lives. It is in such a context that 'recovered memories' may start to emerge. Such memory recall is often characterised by a client looking quite startled, and sometimes behaving as if something is moving or shifting inside his or her body, together with statements such as 'I don't know why this is coming into my mind...', or 'I feel really strange'. It is commonly the case that whatever the person is experiencing is attached to something that has recently been discussed or has taken place. Looking at this can provide a possible way to discuss the new material. Within or outside sessions, the recovery of memories of traumatic experiences often begins with a feeling of disorientation, and headaches are not uncommon.

I have known a few rare occasions when during a session a client has entered a state in which he or she appears to be almost asleep, and in that state describes to me what is being recalled at that precise time – something that had previously been totally repressed. An example of this was a young man who spoke to me in one of his sessions about a particular sensation he was noticing in his hands. He then gradually realised that it was a memory of the texture of the carpet in the hall of his childhood home. During the following session I thought he was falling asleep. I did not disturb him. In his sleep-like state he told me he was on the landing of that same house, that he was very small, and that his legs felt strange. He was clearly puzzled, until he realised that he was tied by his legs to the child safety gate at the top of the stairs. He remembered discovering that he could untie himself, undo the gate, go downstairs, and jump off the bottom step, landing on all fours in his usual way. This immediately explained to him (without any suggestion from me) why he had 'felt' the texture of the carpet the week before. He then remembered running into the kitchen, and he recounted his mother's angry reaction on seeing him there.

Another situation which may arise is that of a client suddenly behaving like a distressed child during the session, pouring out the distress in the voice of the child he or she once was.

There are also occasions when a client may confide to me that he thinks he is going mad. I then ask the client to explain to me exactly what is leading him or her to that conclusion. Careful noting of exactly what stimuli are leading to the experience of the 'going mad feeling' gradually builds up a picture which can then be understood as the nearest the sufferer has ever come to being able to express some highly distressing events of earlier life. For example, I knew someone who had become frightened of a particular name. The name kept flashing in this person's mind more and more, wherever she was, and whether or not she could see it anywhere. Very careful and detailed discussion led to a link between this name and the relationship between siblings. Eventually this led to the memory of an older sibling's very destructive aggression towards this person – a memory which had previously been totally repressed. This kind of process can require a considerable degree of 'emotional detective work'.

I want to write a little here specifically about the recall of sexually abusive events, as there is continuing debate in this area about the veracity of such recall. Clients may confide to me memories of sexual abuse which had never been repressed but which had never yet been shared. In these situations the client has always known what happened, but has never previously felt able to confide. There are occasions where a client will tell me of sexual abuse without realising that that was what he or she had experienced. For example, a woman who was in a residential school as a child told me that a groundsman engaged her in a 'game' in which he 'measured' the length of her torso at the front – inevitably ending up at her genitals. This is of course the kind of trick that can be played on innocent and naïve children. She had felt uncomfortable about the event, but her unease had been brushed off by staff when she tried to say something about it. I confirmed the validity of her feelings.

A female child has two nostrils, two ears, a mouth, an anus and a vagina. A male child has two nostrils, two ears, a mouth and an anus. Unwanted or unexplained penetration of any of these orifices which takes no account of the child's true reaction is experienced by the child as abuse. Inappropriate handling of the genitals of a male child is an intrusion into his person and is also abuse. A friend of mine once confided that her therapist had suggested that her problems stemmed from her father having sexually abused her. She was very upset and distressed by this suggestion, as she believed that her father had never abused her. In a short discussion with her I grasped that she had previously so trusted and respected her therapist that she found this interpretation difficult to challenge as fully as she wished to do. She had come to expect the therapist to be consistently trustworthy. I decided that the best help I could offer was to say that the therapist was probably noticing certain reactions in her that were puzzling, which might have fitted the model of her having been abused by her father. I did not comment upon how this model had been promoted! I then went on to explain how a young child might experience any unexplained intrusion into one of her orifices. I spoke to her about the common use of suppositories in children of her generation, and gave other examples, such as ears being examined roughly, when a child might already be in pain or otherwise distressed. I told her that without proper explanation leading to collaboration between adult and child, the child's body can enter a 'having been violated/assaulted' reaction. My friend was much reassured by my comments.

If a client begins to confide that he or she thinks that he or she has suffered sexual abuse, I will take considerable care to understand precisely what this means to that particular person, as feelings of having been sexually abused can be evoked not only by penetration of orifices other than the genital orifices, but also by inappropriate verbal messages. Although there might be very little distinction in a child's emotional experience between penetrative and non-penetrative sexual abuse, accidental and deliberate verbal sexual abuse, or invasion of orifices other than the genital orifices, it is important to recognise this emotional response for what it is, and then attach it to as precise a memory of events as possible. People need to know the truth and the reality of their experience.

Throughout the process of the discovery of each person's own truth, I show continuous interest as I puzzle with clients about what the sensations, emotions, images and associations may actually mean. In cases where we conclude that penetrative sexual abuse has taken place, it is from a very detailed and broad examination of that person's response to life in a wide range of circumstances which all point to the validity of the recall of the abuse. It is crucially important never to risk a situation where a false 'diagnosis' of sexual abuse is reached, with little or no proper understanding of the person.

In an article about 'Sarah' upon which I was once asked to comment, Sarah was found to have experienced a 'false memory'. However there is no doubt in my mind that she was very distressed about *something*. The nightmares she experienced were one of the indications. Perhaps a significant adult in her childhood had forced upon her certain views and perceptions, and insisted that she incorporate them. Hence, when in this particular case the therapist told her she must have been sexually abused, she found herself back in the same conflict – one where she *had* to believe and accept the views of a person whom she felt to be more powerful than herself.

Many years ago, about a year after the death of my surviving parent – my mother – I myself began to have severe headaches, and started to have flashes of sexual images and of intense anger. This was the beginning of the re-emergence of memories that I had repressed decades earlier when I was a child. I began to record all of this in my daily diary, and slowly over many years the actions of several abusers emerged into my consciousness. I had always had continuous memory of some of the actions of three of my abusers, but what I remembered in later adulthood was 'new' to me.

(ii) Can therapists 'decide' that there has been sexual abuse when none has taken place?

There are therapists who believe that all psychological problems stem from sexual abuse. Such therapists may tell their clients that sexual abuse has taken place, whether or not the client knows or believes it has. This can even lead to a client accusing a parent of abuse, when the only indication of this is through the belief system of the therapist. There are cases where such parents have paid out enormous sums of money in legal fees in order to try to clear themselves.

The False Memory Society was formed as a result of such possibly false accusations. I understand that there have even been some abusers who would join such a society in order to protest innocence.

Other therapists with less rigid beliefs can also suggest to a client a 'diagnosis' of sexual abuse in childhood. I believe such an approach to be unhelpful and misguided. If a client has no conscious memory of sexual abuse, it is either because the client was not abused, or because the memories have been repressed. It is of paramount importance that any therapeutic intervention is based on building a confiding relationship with the therapist, so that any memory recall is entirely authentic to the client, and not 'suggested'.

There are many symptoms, such as problems in eating, which result from sources apart from sexual abuse. There are those who would claim that the existence of eating problems *per se* is sufficient to indicate that sexual abuse has taken place. I myself believe this is not the case.

It is my belief that clients who 'remember sexual abuse' are certainly remembering, or reacting to, something that has been distressing. There are those who are truly remembering events which to the informed observer would appear as sexual abuse. There are also those who have *experienced* certain events as being sexually abusive, and therefore remember them in this frame. The informed observer may not agree that such events were sexually abusive, and this is therefore a grey area. Such a client has most certainly been sexually abused in the sense that this was his or her experience of what took place, but in the law or in the general view of society, that person may not have been sexually abused. Validation of the sufferer's experience is necessary, but with a clear objective understanding of the context. Such distinction and delineation are essential to the resolution of the inherent conflicts. For example, to a child any inadequately explained invasive medical examinations that are performed in a firm, irritable, or even aggressive way can be experienced as abuse. This is an area where feelings of being sexually abused can be generated without anyone other than the child being aware of it.

(iii) Can clients 'remember' sexual abuse that has not happened?

I do believe that it is possible for a client to 'remember' sexual abuse that has not taken place. I believe that this is possible in cases where a client as a young person has been regularly forced to accept beliefs of a parent or carer which are contrary to his or her own view of reality. Hence, later, when a therapist tells such a client that he or she must have been sexually abused, the client feels forced to enter that frame of belief. This situation of the child in relation to the carers, and later in relation to the therapist, constitutes an abuse in itself. Because of the early abuse which was inflicted by distorting the reality of the child, it is then possible for a therapist to enter the sexuality of such a client and distort that client's sense of reality about his or her sexuality. The client can then believe that he or she has been sexually abused, and indeed in a sense this is true, since the *therapist* has behaved in a way that has provoked this.

An adult survivor's perspective

This includes a response to the call for evidence at stage 1 of the Bill SP30 *Protection of Children and Prevention of Sexual Offences (Scotland)*.

PROLOGUE

I parked my car and made my way towards the chiropractic clinic. A man was walking briskly in the same direction, and he kept looking across at me and smiling. I found this strange because at first I did not recognise him; but I soon realised that he too was arriving for treatment, and that I had seen him in the building on a previous visit.

I never looked forward to these appointments – not because I felt that the choice to come was wrong, but because being handled while lying down is never easy for me. This time the apparent friendship of my fellow patient eased the stress. I followed him into the building, exchanged the usual pleasantries at the desk as I collected my file, and then braced myself before making my way to the treatment area, where the radio was emitting its usual wailing sounds. There was an empty seat next to it, which I took while leaning down to silence the noise.

Immediately an unpleasant voice said, 'I was enjoying that.' I realised it was Mr Smile.

I froze inside to stem the tide of agony that would otherwise engulf me, and replied, 'I have permission to turn it off... It makes my head feel very weird.'

Another voice broke in: 'We can't have that.' Was this a sneer or was it genuine? I had no way of knowing as I descended into my inner hell. I clutched my file and read and reread the scribbles on the front page, desperately trying to work out what I could do. I was sinking fast and I had to find a way of appearing 'normal'. I tried to formulate something I could say.

'It's a long story.' I carefully ensured that there was no hint of apology in my tone. 'It involves violence. Not mine.'

His response was entirely silent in its deliberate intensity. I continued to appear to study my file while I sank into the wreckage of my soul. The only coherent thought in my mind was a determination to appear unaffected. I used every fragment of my meagre energy to contain what lay beneath.

His turn came, and I heard him conduct a jolly conversation behind one section of the screen that divided us.

The treatment couch on the other side was free, and I lay on it – face down. The voice continued for a few minutes and then left.

'Hi, how are you?' The chiropractor touched my back lightly.

'Uh…' I said as convincingly as I could.

'You're tense.'

'Um.'

When the familiar routine of manipulations was finished, I staggered through to put on the walking harness before climbing on to one of the treadmills. I was next to him… Claustrophobia. The seconds dragged past as he raced and I tottered.

He left, and a pleasant woman took his place.

As I blundered out of the door I could see that he was turning his car – his glare fixed on the road.

When I arrived home there was bad news about the health of a relative. My frozenness and tension increased. Pain in my back escalated. Glowing coals seemed to have invaded my spinal column, and I lay on ice packs. The pain continued unabated throughout the following day, and I was so exhausted I could hardly stand. It wasn't until the afternoon after that that I began to cry.

I was only too aware that the intensity of this pain was entirely to do with the effect of Mr Smile. The contents of my mind seemed to be boiling with rage and distress. I tried to rehearse scenarios of how I could have handled that situation better, but could find nothing. I should never have let myself lie down and be treated while I was in that state. I could have left without treatment. But what then? I am not convinced that backing away would have been the right decision.

CONSIDERATIONS

The kernel of the problem here is that because I have been severely abused as a child, the behaviour of people like Mr Smile affects me greatly. When

I reflect upon the situation, I can well see that in fact Mr Smile is dysfunctional, but he is not willing to admit it. My problem is that because he was behaving oddly and was refusing to engage with me in a normal way, the child inside me could not separate out the effect of his actions upon me from the actions of early abusers and those people who should have protected me. The consequence of this was that I re-entered the memory of being abused, and my body could only experience the following chiropractic treatment as an abuse session.

I have a hearing defect which makes it very difficult for me to have to listen to musak. At an early stage I had discussed this with the clinic and had arranged that I could turn it off. However, the earliest memory I have of that kind of sound, and a bed, is one of horror – a doctor raping me on a bed, in his home, on his birthday, with many people in the house and a gramophone playing.

Sexual abuse of children is endemic in our society, and those of us who are able should work to address this in a mature way. If I tell the staff at the clinic details of what happened to me as a child it runs the risk of my being seen as someone who is different. There must be many who lie on the treatment couches each day who have suffered similarly. The only difference about me is that throughout my adult life I have tried to find a way of bringing the abuse I suffered into my consciousness, where I then have the option of expressing its existence objectively. Not an easy task, but it is possible, and is necessary if our culture is to advance. When engulfed in the child's feelings, it is very hard to formulate what the adult self can say, but it *can* be done.

An article appeared in *The Times* to mark the sixtieth anniversary of the liberation of Auschwitz. I learned that there is a manual – *Caring for Aging Holocaust Survivors* – which explains survivors' reactions to various 'triggers' so that medical staff can understand. For example, showers evoke gas chambers.

For those of us who have been sexually abused as children, we have to know our own 'manual' by heart. My own first 'entry' – carved in my mind – is a visit to a slaughterhouse. This was part of my degree course when I was nineteen. It took many years before I could see that desperate despairing animals having holes made in them in the presence of blood was not only a horror in its own right, but was also an image through which my child was 'remembering'.

The 'manual' gives us power. Life is not easy, but can only improve through knowing ourselves more deeply. And then the way forward is to harness that knowledge and put it across effectively – for the benefit of ourselves and society.

Last November provided me with an opportunity to contribute to society's understanding of certain aspects of the sexual abuse that is endemic in our society. My submission appears below.

Protection of Children and Prevention of Sexual Offences (Scotland) Bill SP30 – response to the call for evidence at stage 1.

Submission by Mrs A M Maslin

30 November 2004

1.

Thank you to Cathy Jamieson for introducing this Bill – which is an attempt to reduce the likelihood of harm to individuals in society (and society as a whole) by certain specific sexualised behaviour of adults towards children. It is an important signal in our society that we are moving further in the direction of addressing the complexities of inappropriate behaviour towards our developing young.

Although it is a small step in the morass of change that needs to take place to protect and nourish our children, it is a significant one. It takes place in parallel with progress in other areas such as improving levels of pollution in the air we breathe – of which a ban on smoking in public places will play a part.

2.

I am concerned about the protection of children who in their own homes may be groomed by family members or other relatives.

A conversation I had with an experienced police officer included the distress of that officer on having to return to her home a female child who had disclosed to the police the sexual abuse she was suffering from her mother's new partner. The child's mother had said that the child was lying.

I learned that this kind of situation was not an isolated event.

Please will the Committee consider this area very carefully while discussing the final provisions of the Bill.

3.

I am concerned about the safety of people such as members of teaching staff in school, who may become the focus of a malicious complaint by a child or children under the age of sixteen.

I have read several reports in the national press of cases where teachers' careers have been ruined by wrongful accusations of sexualised behaviour or sexual harassment towards young people.

Please will the Committee consider this aspect when discussing the final provisions of the Bill.

4.

I am concerned to ensure that children are protected from grooming activities carried out by an adult member of the same sex or a member of the opposite sex, or indeed any adult couple or group.

(I refer to paragraph 15 of the policy memorandum, but am not clear if it covers the matter to which I refer.)

Please will the Committee ensure that the Bill provides for this.

5.

I am concerned about rehabilitation of offenders.

In recent years I made attempts to identify schemes in prisons that were enabling prisoners to return to society with some confidence in all parties that such people would not re-offend. I understand that best results are obtained in cases where offenders come to understand the roots of their problems (which are frequently to do with emotional deprivation, distress and isolation), are then able to understand the damage caused by their wrong actions, and are opened to being helped to relate to others in society in mutually supportive ways. I could not find any such schemes operating in Scotland.

Please will the Committee consider this area very carefully.

6.

I am concerned about measures that could be taken in society that are likely to lead to a reduction in the likelihood of adults seeking out children for contact that manifests as sexual gratification.

(i) In a society where much of the advertising is driven by sexualised postures, our citizens are bombarded daily by false links between sexual activity or seductive behaviour and other things. That in itself is a kind of grooming process. For example, I enclose two advertisements that appeared in the national press, each of which is from what would be regarded a reputable organisation – BUPA and Stobo Castle (copies attached).

(ii) It appears to me that in our society girls are being encouraged to dress and behave like miniature adults at a younger and younger age. This can include behaviour that can be construed as seductive.

For example, I refer to an article about the winning singer and the song lyrics of the recent Junior Eurovision Song Contest (copy attached). The title of the song is 'I'd rather be dead than plain.' The lyrics include the words 'It helps to give me rhythm, I'm a real little mover'. The winner is 9 years old. It appears to me that the song contest itself is a kind of grooming.

Although this kind of contrived adult behaviour in children is not a reason for excusing the behaviour of offenders, it is something that we should look at very carefully. It is easy to see how ease of access to alcohol for those who are struggling with that particular addiction is an issue that we need to address. The person who uses alcohol to attempt to numb a sense of inner deprivation has much in common with those who use sexual activity for the same purpose, and who are therefore vulnerable to 'seduction' by repeated sensory insults from a plethora of sources.

(iii) I believe that it should be made mandatory that all schools provide not only sexual education but also relationship education. I notice that young people are struggling to understand the real meaning of relationship, and, aided by the media, are frequently confusing the excitement of sexual activity with real affection, understanding and commitment.

Please will the Committee consider very seriously all parts of section 6 of my response.

7.

I am deeply concerned that false attitudes about sexual impulses and sexual activity of adults towards children have become endemic in our society.

At a conference on all kinds of abuse of children I overheard a group of men discussing the section on sexual abuse. 'Let's face it,' said one to the others, 'we all think our daughters look amazing, but you don't do anything except let them know they are stunning.' I admired this man for his honesty, correctness and directness of speech.

However, at a writers' group, a male member wrote an interesting short story in which a man encountered a homeless thirteen year old girl, who he then invited to a café for a hot drink. The male members of the group nudged each other, tittering, and one said, '*We* know what happens next! Hee hee.' Before I left I spoke to the author of the (incomplete) story, saying that I hoped that the main character would continue to behave appropriately towards the girl. He looked at his feet and did not reply. I have not attended the group since that time, and I still search my mind about what else I could have said and done.

These two examples demonstrate the difference between the safe and entirely appropriate attitude of a father (or person acting in that capacity) and the attitude of the potential offender (be it a stranger or a neighbour or a relative).

Please will the Committee be aware of this important area.

8.

For the secure development of a child, his or her primary emotional connection needs to be with a safe and trusted adult person – who is either the mother or someone who is in that position in relation to the child. I am concerned by the tendency in our society to encourage situations where a young child is required to trust relative strangers (e.g. while in nursery care), often with very little 'bridging' of the situation (i.e. where the child would experience warm and regular communication between his or her parent(s) and the nursery staff). This surely is creating the basis of vulnerability in children to the kind of grooming process to which the Bill refers, since it signals that significant intimate care can be provided at a location remote from the home base, both geographically and emotionally.

Please will the Committee consider this serious matter very carefully.

9.

With regard to the provisions of the Bill that would make it an offence to expose children to images of sexual or sexualised activity, I draw the Committee's attention again to the gross sexualisations that appear in advertising. For example, I consider the image of David Beckham's naked torso together with a razor that is being advertised on hoardings at the moment to involve sexual innuendo.

A news item in the *Scotsman* (26 November 2004) read as follows: 'Pornographic images in magazines and newspapers, on public transport and on the Internet have been blamed for violence against women in Scotland. Yesterday was a UN international day of action to eliminate such violence.'

I am also deeply concerned about the exposure of children to sexual and sexualised images on TV during the screening of advertising and various programmes. I am at a loss as to how the provisions of the Bill can regulate this.

Please will the Committee consider these matters (paragraph 9) very carefully.

10.

I write not only as an adult who resides in Scotland, but also as a therapist who is concerned with the treatment of emotional problems and relationship problems, some of which stem directly from certain situations in childhood where sexually abusive behaviour has been involved. I do have personal experience of being sexually abused as a child.

As a published author I was approached to write a novel that would be helpful to girls in the age group 9-15 years. The book will be published early next year, and it contains much to help girls to maintain and develop good relationships with responsible adults and with one another. This is the basis from which they develop their own sense of self, which includes a growing sense of appropriate sexual attitudes. This area is fundamental to reducing the vulnerability of that age group to sexual seduction by disturbed adults, including those who use the media to groom our children. (I can make an electronic copy or an A4 hard copy of the book available to the Committee.)

Addictions and 'cold turkey'

Much is written about addiction to substances such as tobacco, alcohol and illegal drugs. Recent studies in Scotland suggest that one in thirteen adults are addicted to alcohol, and that one in fifty are addicted to heroin. We also have those who become addicted to prescription drugs. The word 'addiction' may conjure up an image of people who are showing obvious symptoms of agitation before being able to reach each 'dose' or 'fix'. There is evidence that people can be attached in this way even to substances such as tea and coffee. It is well known that there are certain substances, or constituents of substances, which react in the human body in such a way as to establish quickly an increasing need for that substance for the person to feel okay.

The term 'addiction' can be applied loosely to include any situation where a person feels an overwhelming, regular, urgent need or 'craving' for a particular thing. Here I would wish to include activities. For example, there are those who develop an addiction to exercise, and there are those whose exercising is driven by a fear of putting on weight – leading to gym attendances which in themselves can become an addiction. There are those who vomit, those who shout, those who stare at TV, those who make extra visits to doctors, and those who even undergo repeated surgical interventions, to an extent that can be seen as being addictive behaviour.

What is it that a person is seeking by their urgent reaching for a substance or activity? It is my understanding that each one is driven by the belief that it will result in their 'feeling better' – i.e. a reduction of intensely difficult feelings. However, such relief is only temporary, and therefore requires indefinitely repeated 'doses' or events; and the size of the dose may need to be increased to produce the desired 'relief'. R D Laing wrote of a man who derived intense comfort from his proximity to a domestic fire; but discovering that as time went on he required a more and more intense experience of the heat, he moved closer and closer until finally his body was endangered.

Taking in food is a daily necessity. Food needs to be eaten in response to hunger. In our society there is currently more food than we need. Certain flavourings and colourings in food, together with promotional skills, can lead people to eat solely to obtain a 'pleasure' feeling, rather than to satisfy basic physical hunger. I would go as far as to say that children in our society are exposed to advertising which promotes the illusion that one's sense of self is to a significant degree dependent upon consumption of food. There are foods which have been highly processed, then further prepared and presented in a way that provokes and encourages a perceived need to consume them. There is a mass of evidence which indicates that regular consumption of such foods leads to gradual deterioration in health. The EPIC study of nutrition and health, begun in 1993, has clearly shown that for the health of the nation much promotion should focus on fruit and vegetables.

The healthy development of the sense of self within the human infant is dependent upon the infant receiving adequate input of appropriate responses from carers. What happens if the input is inadequate, or actively damaging? The infant is left with emotional hungers. What happens to these hungers? In the life of the child circumstances may arise which belatedly meet some of these. What happens if none are met? A person carries the effect of early deprivation or damage, and frequently has no conscious knowledge of this, and therefore has no words to describe or express it. Here then we have a situation where a person may well feel a hunger or a drive or a need for something, and that drive can become attached to any focus which seems as if it meets the need. The person feels better when fixing on such a focus (e.g. use of drugs, alcohol, swallowing or vomiting of food, or 'driven' exercise regimes), but finds that regular doses are required to continue the 'better' feeling, and that these doses can be needed in increasing quantity. The sufferer can even reach a situation where the need, and therefore the dose, becomes almost continuous. Unresolved problems from very early life often lead to attachments to sucking behaviours such as smoking, drinking from bottles, excessive sexual activity, and also a desire for intensely sweet stimuli.

When it becomes apparent to the sufferer, or to others, that the use or overuse of a substance or activity is out of balance with the rest of his or her life, then it is seen as a problem. But it is not necessarily the sufferer's relationship with the particular focus that is the problem. Take for example a certain 'binge drinker' who anaesthetises himself thus from time to time. Careful examination of that person's life might reveal that there are some factors which have commonly presented in the days prior to a 'binge'. If a person is deemed to be 'alcoholic', Alcoholics Anonymous would advise total abstention as the only solution. (I should make it clear that I am not in any way against total abstention.) However, a concerned observer might see that before each binge, the sufferer had good reason to feel very intense unbearable emotions which he does not understand, or of which he may be entirely unaware. Instead he has reached urgently for alcohol – a route which is to his obvious detriment. If total abstention is the only focus or goal, the sufferer does not receive the help and encouragement that he needs to access his unbearable emotions. Since this self-knowledge is a prerequisite of discovering effective ways of addressing situations that provoke such emotions, without it a sufferer could find it very difficult, or impossible, to diminish the urge to reach for alcohol.

Another outcome of abstention without understanding can be that the sufferer, in his struggle to stop reaching for alcohol, becomes addicted to hearing an inner command to 'concentrate upon successfully achieving total abstention'. This is demonstrably a less damaging addiction. A further example concerns the person who transfers his addiction to alcohol to an addiction to attending AA meetings – finding ways of attending as many groups as possible, and over-promoting AA doctrine. Perhaps the groups are then experienced as the 'good family' that the sufferer never had. The change has the great benefit of removing alcohol from the sufferer's life, and of his potentially being closer to caring people. However, his improvement could be further advanced if he were assisted to identify and examine the impulses which gave rise to the over-consumption of alcohol in the first place. The great benefit of this is to enable the person to redirect such impulses in ways that are authentic to his true self. If these matters are addressed, the likelihood of the sufferer returning to alcohol addiction, or of his becoming addicted to other substances, is at least reduced, and at best removed.

The process of identifying and examining intense impulses and their associated emotions is likely to be very painful. While doing so, the sufferer may even feel physical 'withdrawal' symptoms similar to those experienced in the 'cold turkey' of drug withdrawal. I knew a young nurse who had previously been addicted to morphine, who later experienced again the symptoms of 'morphine withdrawal' when examining the deep emotional material she had originally suppressed by its use. This took place many months after she had last used the drug. 'Cold turkey', 'drying out' and 'withdrawal' are words that are very familiar to those concerned with the immediate aftermath of drug withdrawal. It is important to recognise that, as in the case of the nurse, these terms can also be applied to the period of time in which a person begins to recognise the emotional distress, the suppression of which had led to addictive behaviours.

A consultant paediatrician once said to me that he had patients on diamorphine (heroin) in hospital, but discontinued it completely at discharge. He made the point that if heroin is used as a part of proper nursing care and concern, then the patient need not develop a craving for it.

There is some concern in our society that people can become addicted to visiting counsellors. In cases where a client shows symptoms of 'over-dependence' or addiction to a drug or activity, the true role of the counsellor is to help the client to identify and examine the emotional material which is driving this behaviour. As this is elucidated, the client develops ways of relating to the world that are right for him, so that he no longer feels the need to 'cling'. In the course of this process the counsellor must allow feelings of dependency to be recognised and discussed. If not, visits to the counsellor can become an addiction, masked or overt – the client clinging on to the visits because his real need is not being addressed. In that entirely unsatisfactory situation there are even cases where a client can incessantly *talk about* feelings as a way of holding on to the counsellor, instead of being helped to look at the emotions associated with the problems that lie within. The counsellor has a responsibility to provide help to identify and recognise the client's painful feelings, and to offer interpretations where appropriate. The help must result in aiding the client in the process of handling emotional states in such a way as to be able to express them appropriately and effectively, being confident of the correct expression for each context.

What is going wrong?
by Dr W N Taylor

I am concerned about the prevalence of social unrest in our society, particularly among young people, and I would like to write some notes in an attempt to understand it.

There is a tendency these days for physical sexual relationship among young people to become 'normalised'. This accompanies an increasing emphasis placed on sexuality in ever-extending aspects of life. Attractive objects are described as 'sexy'. Even Government documents are being 'sexed up'. Provocative images are everywhere. Older children cannot escape this influence, and are often unable to handle it in a balanced way. They are encouraged to learn about 'safe sex' before they have been able to grasp the realities of loving relationship. Contraceptives are readily available to them. Inevitably younger children are drawn in, and are influenced either thoughtlessly or deliberately by the entertainment industry and advertising. In such cases a balanced understanding cannot be expected, and damaging confusion can result. This imposes a huge responsibility upon those adults who have the care of small children entrusted to them, to keep sex in its rightful place. I fear that many of those adults have themselves been affected in early life by the adverse influences to which I have referred, and this problem should be recognised. It has deep roots and serious consequences. Emotionally damaged children make inadequate parents or carers, who in turn pass the problem on, and a chain of pathology is established. In the case of schoolchildren, abstinence is often not advocated as normal behaviour. Children should surely be led to believe that they do not have to *act* on the sexual feelings they have, but this is not always done. On the contrary, to the youngster virginity can be a sign of low standing among peers, and one is led to assume that this state of affairs is not questioned, if not actually approved of, by the adults in charge.

These issues are part of a wider change in our culture that has accelerated from the post-war period of social 'liberation'. There has been a weakening of family bonds, and changes in the interpretation of parental responsibility. There has arisen a clear choice between personal 'freedom' to do what one wants to satisfy personal ambition (e.g. in lifestyle and career), and the responsibilities of parenthood. On the one hand, both women and men direct their energies into activities that are only indirectly (if at all) related to the emotional needs of their children, and on the other hand there is the view that if you have children they should come first. If, as so often happens, personal choices come first, the children tend to become something to be coped with – handed over to other available adults or professional child-minders, so as not to interfere with what has become the 'real' business of life. The older institution of the Public School has remained for those who can afford it. So instead of being supported in expressing his real anxieties, the infant, toddler or early adolescent is made to suppress these feelings as best he can. His emotional needs are overlooked, denied, scoffed at or argued away – potentially with serious consequences. A child cannot become a secure and confident complete person without experiencing these attributes through a close and loving contact with adults who are themselves secure and confident in relation to him or her. In this relationship the child absorbs as his own the quality of a parental attitude to him. How else can respect for others arise in a child? He cannot grow up in an emotional desert. He grows through relationship. These qualities develop within him from his experience of loving respect and security within a nurturing attachment, which puts him first in the meeting of his real needs. It must be noted that this relationship is established uniquely with the primary carer – ideally the natural mother. A child cannot benefit emotionally if he is shuttled around between different carers. He is merely bewildered by this, and at a deep level insecure, no matter how genuinely dedicated the other carers are. I sometimes think that some people understand this more with their pets than with their children!

If such a unique maternal relationship is not adequately provided, the child is to that extent deprived – handicapped in trying to become a whole human being, lacking adequate emotional food, and therefore unable to grow as he should. This opens the way to many personal and social problems, and many children find themselves on this problematic route. It can take different forms according to circumstances, but inadequate relationship lies at the root of it. Currently a problem of obesity is recognised. Children are eating excessively (often junk food) as a substitute for missing emotional sustenance, and there are many other behavioural and health problems arising from that source.

If a child has not grown up in real relationship of the kind described, he or she has no inner sense of security with others. He cannot sense 'goodness' in them because he has no root experience of goodness, and cannot feel it, however much he may believe in it or intellectually grasp that there must be such a thing. A secure child carries within himself the awareness of being a proper person, through having been treated as a proper person, so incorporating essentially good values from the good parent who nurtured him. If this has not happened, the feeling of being 'good' is lacking – despite anything he may be taught through his rational mind. Here we are not dealing with thinking or logic, but the deeper belief of feeling. I am alarmed at the increase in numbers of children diagnosed as suffering from Asperger's syndrome.

What are the consequences of this deprivation? They will come from the young person's attempts to build a life for himself, by trying to find some way of coping with the vacuum. He has to try to find elsewhere an emotional satisfaction that will give his life some sense of meaning. His social environment offers many and varied possibilities, some of which we have mentioned above; and because whatever the resulting substitute behaviour is, it deals with a deep and very basic need that tends to feel essential and to become addictive. Of course many emotionally handicapped children fortunately do find ways that are socially acceptable if not wholly adequate; but the less fortunate get carried away all too easily by a prevailing culture which is anything but desirable. Sexual behaviour is an obvious way to seek emotional satisfaction, and the provocative stimuli are all around; but because in this context it is not associated with a real loving relationship, it is perpetually unsatisfying – so the search becomes promiscuous, and leads to addiction. Highly available alcohol is another common false substitute for an absent comforting attachment – again addictive, emotionally as well as physically – and drug addiction comes into the same category. Apart from these, we find all kinds of social misbehaviour among young people resulting from the fact that they cannot find a substitute for a missing relationship that gives them any peace. They go about angry with the world. In their hearts they are angry babies whose mother never satisfied them. We can see the obvious connection here with crime. Such emotional states can very easily result in robbery and violence, crimes of envy and jealousy and much other antisocial behaviour.

Another relevant issue in the forefront today is obesity, which has acquired the status of a disease, to be fought with drugs and/or diet and exercise. No doubt faulty diet and overeating are involved, but the important thing to look at is the cause of this behaviour, rather than to impose instructions and conditions that can be resisted or disregarded. Perhaps we should look at the problem in the light of what I have said already about addiction, and the underlying importance of faulty relationship in the individual's background. Perhaps the higher incidence of obesity among the underprivileged is not solely due to junk food, but also, and perhaps primarily, to disturbed relationships in an overstressed and anxious community – a serious social problem.

Now there is the much publicised 'yob culture', which is frequently associated with binge drinking. This has been taken seriously by the Government, and through this the police have been involved specifically to deal with antisocial behaviour – implying that it is something to be deterred by punishment, control and public humiliation. This approach would seem to me to provoke bitter resentment and further aggressive behaviour. What else could we expect? I believe it would be more effective to examine the causes of aggressive behaviour – in other words to regard it as another manifestation of failed relationships between the offenders and the rest of society. They are behaving like neglected or unwanted children, who will clearly not be 'cured' by further rejection. I cannot be drawn into proposing a cure aimed at the offenders. That is a political question. But I think that it should be based upon the right premises. The real problem is the parents, and other adults responsible for their upbringing, from whom the children have no option but to learn how to behave.

I would repeat that a very great deal of social unrest has its origin in the absence or loss of necessary nurturing relationship during infancy, carried on throughout childhood and adolescence, when the basic experiences needed for secure personality growth are laid down. An unfulfilling (and therefore hopeless) substitute is then sought at a time that is too late developmentally for reparation, and the substitute sources that offer themselves tend to exploit the tragedy for financial gain. Only a really secure caring relationship over time might help to make things more tolerable, but because in the adolescent it is occurring at a time too late to be properly internalised, such a relationship would need to be permanent – or rupture would then be a disaster.

The problem of what can be done is certainly formidable, but the first step has to be a general understanding of what it is. Here I have proposed a psychological theory, based upon what is known about the psychopathology of human development. The concepts of such theory, dare I say, may themselves have been modified these days by the prevailing culture – and, I suspect, may now follow less personal, more materialistic concepts that match the current social norms. Of course there must be other views on other premises. But what is needed at the moment is a serious interest, and serious discussion, involving as many sources as possible. This would surely be a hopeful starting point.

Where do we find the other premises? One that overlaps the above is that of morality and spiritual values. A new person is born into the world physically from the mother, with whom he remains an extension as it were, throughout his infancy. Later he becomes autonomous through the development of his genetic capabilities. But he is also a being endowed with life, with all its potentialities and values; and these assert themselves progressively as autonomy increases, leading to the necessity for his making choices. He is a descendant of Adam, and carries the potentialities of both good and evil in his nature. Therein a struggle could arise between self-will and what he discovers of moral good. But this discovery is not necessarily the imposed rules of adults. There can also be an appeal to an inner sense of what later comes to be felt as goodness – a moral value. The tendency these days is to look on moral values epistemologically, as knowledge acquired by learning, rather than existentially, as a given quality in the human soul. These concepts are matters of opinion, but the choice is important. If goodness is learned, morality would appear to be dependent on the custom of the age, although here a consistent attitude to religion could play a part, pointing to an existential component. In our country this latter attitude is waning, and with it an acceptance of the spiritual value of the human person. So the choice between right and wrong is reduced to a matter of obedience or disobedience to human authority: 'Everybody can be good if they want to be. If they don't, they must be coerced into changing their ways.' There is little if any recognition of an inner knowledge of goodness that has been blocked, but which can be freed by kind and caring relationship. Is it not so that all persons were innocent once? What have we done to them? Perhaps we have to go back in time to find out.

If a child has to be taught what is good and what is bad, it implies that his mind is, morally, a blank slate. My contention is that if he has *experienced* an early loving relationship with another person he has, in his being, an awareness of the reality of 'goodness' which he does not owe to didactic moral teaching. And he feels 'badness' as an infringement of his natural state, which enters consciousness as unease or distress. Experience within that state can be the basis for discovering the moral values of right and wrong, by building up an understanding of these matters in line with the deeper understanding that is already there. This contrasts with the didactic practice that stamps these values as foreign concepts upon a child who may lack the inner assimilated experience to enable proper acceptance and true understanding. Such a child may go on to seek ways of circumventing these learned principles and simply do what he wants, through lack of the deep inner feeling of rightness – from which such behaviour could not arise.

This consideration leads naturally to the topic of guilt. Freud's idea of a superego derived from a dominant father is clearly based on the 'blank slate' idea of moral behaviour, which some might call materialistic, or even atheistic. It presumes no pre-existing source which can be contacted by loving experience. Freud's concept of the inner self was a raging force demanding gratification, which he appropriately called the 'Id' (literally the Thing). This force was hammered into the shape demanded by social culture by the child's domineering father, internalised as what he called the 'Super-ego' (something superior to the self). The force exerted by the Super-ego on the Id gives rise to guilt – for wanting an inbred satisfaction that was forbidden. In this scheme Good is simply the absence of Bad, and seems to have no other basis. This view would seem to be primitive in the extreme, missing out what seems to me to be the essential core of humanity. In a sense, morality has disappeared in a system of domination and guilt, in which the person has no moral choice – simply obedience, to avoid pain. It may be that Freud's ideas arose from the concept of the Jewish God, with whom goodness arose from obedience and sacrifice. To continue the theological argument further, one can compare the ancient Hebrew scheme with the vastly different teaching of the New Testament, where the Christian doctrine that God is Love is consistent with the developmental ideas propounded above about the origin in love of goodness and right behaviour.

I have heard it said that a child nurtured to be secure and happy will consider himself to be the centre of the earth, and treat others with disdain. This is nonsense. That child will treat the other in accordance with his internalised image as an equal in mutually caring relationship. Alas, he may find out later, to his sorrow, that in the world at large very different responses have to be experienced and adapted to, because there exist in the world powerful and disturbing influences that would appear to arise from a very basic prevalence of the 'unloved' state (to use the above terminology) in humanity as a whole. The exercise of power and coercion, either brutally, or under the guise of altruism, by governments and individuals, has percolated throughout human life from time immemorial. It is as if the world at large were behaving like an insecure unloved child – and as if civilisation were an attempt to seek another way to find peace. Not a very satisfactory way, as history shows. I seem to deduce from this that the mass of humanity feels exiled from a loving relationship that alone would bring peace. The gates of Eden have closed behind it.

This inference draws the mind inexorably to a theological premise. We appear to be talking about humanity's alienation from God, and this in turn introduces the topic of original sin, since the absolute love of God is constant by definition. 'Man's first disobedience...' begins *Paradise Lost*. Psychologists have considered this as a metaphor for the child's transition from the innocence of infancy to the self-conscious choices facing the early adolescent in his emergent independence – no longer subject entirely to the adults' will, but faced with responsibility for his own life, errors of judgement and all. This is a tempting analogy. The sticking-point is the conception of *sin*, with the implication that growing up is evil. Ancient Judaism did regard sexuality, the hallmark of puberty, as impure, and surrounded it with strict prohibitions as if it were sinful, and this tendency has remained in the Christian tradition. As a result, much emotional disturbance and neurosis has arisen, and the modern emphasis has moved somewhat away from sin to pathology. But a degree of prohibition has remained, although seen now as arising from wrongs of hygiene rather than immorality. It is this situation that has now brought about a virtual removal of prohibition. But the pendulum has swung too far, and I have been pleading for a return to continence as a *normal* condition of loving care prevailing in growing up, that would entail health and hygiene as a consequence.

I must return to my conviction that it is on the health of *relationship* between persons that the physical, emotional and moral health of individuals and of society, and of the human race as a whole, depends. And healthy relationship begins in the family, between parents and child. This is arguably the most important thing in life, and we have been allowing it to become sidelined. This, I think, is what has gone wrong.

Dr W Norman Taylor MB, ChB, DPM   24 November 2004

For other titles from Augur Press

please visit

www.augurpress.com

Lightning Source UK Ltd.
Milton Keynes UK
UKOW04f1141210514

232060UK00001B/3/P